⤞ CLOISTER ⤝
ABBOT

&

PRECINCT

✦ CLOISTER ✦
ABBOT
&
PRECINCT
IN
MEDIEVAL MONASTERIES

✦ MICHAEL THOMPSON ✦

TEMPUS

First published 2001

PUBLISHED IN THE UNITED KINGDOM BY:

Tempus Publishing Ltd
The Mill, Brimscombe Port
Stroud, Gloucestershire GL5 2QG
www.tempus-publishing.com

PUBLISHED IN THE UNITED STATES OF AMERICA BY:

Tempus Publishing Inc.
2 Cumberland Street
Charleston, SC 29401
1-888-313-2665
www.arcadiapublishing.com

Tempus books are available in France and Germany
from the following addresses:

Tempus Publishing Group   Tempus Publishing Group
21 Avenue de la République   Gustav-Adolf-Straße 3
37300 Joué-lès-Tours   99084 Erfurt
FRANCE   GERMANY

British Library Cataloguing in Publication Data.
A catalogue record for this book is available from the British Library.

ISBN 0 7524 1936 6

Typesetting and origination by Tempus Publishing.
PRINTED AND BOUND IN GREAT BRITAIN

Contents

Battle Abbey, gatehouse, licensed 1338, outside in 1818. Only the central tower is fourteenth-century with the twelfth-century gate to its right. John Coney

Preface

Having recently discussed medieval bishops' houses (Thompson, 1998) my attention inevitably turned to the housing of bishops' fellow lords spiritual, the medieval abbots and priors. The resources available, either written or architectural, do not allow anything like the same kind of treatment and so my familiarity with extensive monastic remains exposed in the 'heroic' inter-war years of the Office of Works (Thompson, 1977) made it appear necessary to work on a broader canvas. It seemed particularly useful to look at monasticism in less insular terms than is customary in this country: so the first two chapters of the book have strayed widely from Egypt to Europe and only in the last three chapters of the book has the subject been confined largely to England. The prime interest in this brief work is still with buildings but perhaps treated a little more historically than usual. The author is not trying to teach so much as to explore for his own satisfaction, as much as that of the reader, to pursue those aspects of the subject often ignored but of great interest. The reader may find it helpful to read the chapter entitled 'Conclusion' first as forming a summary of the book.

A work of this kind cannot be written without relying on many others. I have had the advantage of being able to cull monastic licences to crenellate from the list of Charles Coulson. John Schofield has most kindly made additions for me to the list of abbots' houses in London. The Egypt Exploration Society has told me of references to fieldwork on the sites of the monasteries of Pachomius in the Thebaid. Lorna Price and her husband Robert P. Dittmer made the photographs of the illustrations especially from the first volume of the great work by Horn and Born on the St Gall plan. Dr Glyn Coppack kindly allowed me to use several of his monastic plans. The other illustrations have been drawn from the publications of many workers in the field, both past and present, to whom I must express my gratitude for allowing their use. The bibliography at the end names many of them. The ground photographs are all from my wife's camera, and I am greatly indebted to her.

Michael Thompson
Cambridge, 2001

Acknowledgements

Grateful acknowledgement is made to the following bodies for permission to use material for illustrations, acknowledgement to individuals being made in the figure captions. Photographic reproduction of the St Gall plan is the copyright of Stifts-bibliotek St Gallen, Cod Sang 1092.

Figures **2** & **3** University of California Press; **5** Nelson; **7** Canterbury Archaeological Trust; **8**, **9**, **27**, **29**, **42** Society of Antiquaries of London; **10**, **37**, **41**, **44** English Heritage (Crown Copyright); **11**, **28**, **33**, **49**, Royal Archaeological Institute; **12**, **13**, **14** Lorna Price, Friday Harbour, Washington State; **21**, **22**, **24** Cambridge University Air Photographic Collection; **23** Norwich City Council; **26** Cadw, Welsh Historic Monuments (Crown Copyright); **35** Thoresby Society; **36** Norfolk and Norwich Archaeological Society; **45** Yorkshire Archaeological Society; **46**, **47**, British Archaeological Association.

List of illustrations

1 Before the cloister

Before the cloister

The tourist in Russia will almost certainly visit monasteries for there is something of a revival following the Soviet repression. His first impression from the outside is of a substantial fortification, no doubt needed in the face of so many enemies on the steppe, and the more so in that there were no castles, the monasteries around Moscow acting to some extent as substitutes. An outer enclosure though not so heavily fortified is common to all monasteries within which the normal liturgical life of the monks could proceed undisturbed by the world outside. Of more immediate concern to us are the arrangements of buildings within the enclosure.

Within a Russian monastery there is no fixed plan for the buildings although the main church may occupy a central position with other churches at different points, the refectory being below one of them. Two-storied churches are quite normal in Russia. The *laura* containing the cells in which the monks sleep is commonly set against the enclosing wall. There is no question of a cloister that is the buildings being set out in ranges around a square courtyard attached to the western arm, the nave, of the church as in western monasteries. The stubby centralised Russian church would not indeed lend itself to such an arrangement. Not only the liturgy, the form of worship, but the buildings in which it is performed are wholly different from the west.

The Russian church was ultimately derived from Greek Byzantium so attention may be turned to the 20 or so monasteries on the peninsula projecting south-east from Macedonia known as Mount Athos. Comparison of the plans which have been published in one book (Capuani, 1988) shows that no two are exactly alike. The churches, more than one within each enclosure, are too short for a cloister to be attached and none exist. In the Great Laura, the most important, which retains features from the eleventh century, the church is so set that it confronts a great T-shaped refectory in a dramatic fashion, a fairly clear indication of what were regarded as the most important buildings in the monastery. None of the others closely follow this layout (**1**).

It is not necessary to pursue this further for it is evident that monasticism of eastern or Greek origin may have similar ultimate objectives but employs not only a very different liturgy but also has a very different architecture that does not encompass a cloister in the sense that is used here. This is in no way to detract from the value of these establishments; a cloister does not improve the form of monasticism although it may influence what may be described as its ethos. The cloister then was something created in the west and at some point west and east parted company. By going back to the origin of Christian monasteries the sequence can be followed until the cloister appears; so that is how we shall proceed.

PIANTA DEL MONASTERO

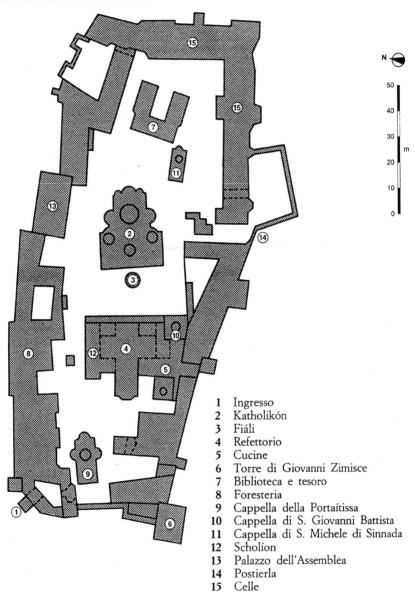

1 Ingresso
2 Katholikón
3 Fiáli
4 Refettorio
5 Cucine
6 Torre di Giovanni Zimisce
7 Biblioteca e tesoro
8 Foresteria
9 Cappella della Portaítissa
10 Cappella di S. Giovanni Battista
11 Cappella di S. Michele di Sinnada
12 Scholíon
13 Palazzo dell'Assemblea
14 Postierla
15 Celle

1 Mount Athos, plan of Great Lura. Note main church (2), refectory (4), gatehouse (8), cells (15). Massimo Capuani

St Pachomius (AD 292-346)

Christianity was already widespread in the Roman Empire in the third century AD when the intermittent periods of persecution, especially under Diocletian (AD 284-305), caused many Christians to flee into the desert, particularly the Western desert, south-west of Alexandria, the great cultural capital of the time. The hermit-like life that such refugees lived and the form of mysticism bred in the desert with which the name of St Anthony (251-356) is especially associated aroused much admiration at the time and has done so ever since. In the Thebaid region of Upper Egypt, on the Nile bank north of Thebes and some 400 miles upstream from Alexandria (Cairo did not yet exist) a much more fixed and permanent development took place that had incalculable influence on the spiritual life of the later church.

Pachomius, unlike other early Fathers, did not write a large theological work and he is known to us from Greek and Coptic *Lives* written shortly after his death and from his Rule written down a little later in the fourth century (Rousseau, 1985). Unfortunately all his monasteries with one important exception have vanished with so little trace left behind that only approximate sites are known (**2 & 3**).

Pachomious was conscripted into the Roman army and while he was in prison had his first encounter with Christians, for he was still a pagan. On his release from the army he was converted to Christianity but his attempts to form a group of disciples were unsuccessful. Advised by a hermit, Palamon, to create a more permanent community he chose the site of an abandoned settlement at Tabannisis in *c*.AD 318. The etymology of the Coptic name of the place is regarded as 'sanctuary of Isis' so the site may well have been already hallowed. He did not of course use the word 'monastery', but the term used in the written sources is *koinonia,* which was applied to Tabennisis and all subsequent foundations as well as all of them together. It simply means 'community'. The number of foundations grew to eight with two separate foundations for women, scattered along the Nile, on both banks. According to one of the Coptic *Lives* communication between the monasteries was by boat. The initial foundation at Tabennisis was soon replaced by Phbow (Coptic, Arabic Fow el-Qibli) as a main centre.

Nearly all features of later monasticism were present: a uniform habit or dress, a regular schedule of work and prayer, communal meals, daily meetings like chapter meetings, a sort of Order created by uniformity over the whole group of houses situated at some distance from each other, importance of literacy (recruits who might be pagan were taught to read prayers and Scripture). The Rule itself was perhaps oral at this stage and only written down after the death of Pachomius, later in the fourth century. It is the living of life according to a Rule that distinguishes the religious — monks — from secular or pastoral clergy.

The monasteries evidently contained elaborate buildings apart from the church which might have survived in the open desert, but in the flood plain of the Nile floods and intensive agriculture have removed almost all visible vestiges of brick (adobe) buildings or enclosures except for the church at Phbow. At Phbow, where monolithic Roman columns from the basilica (main church) are scattered over the surface, there was evidence that the remains were subject to seasonal flooding before the construction of the Aswan dam

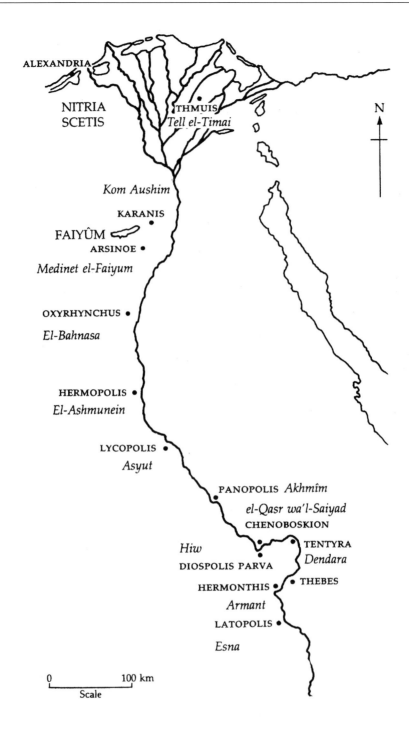

ALEXANDRIA

NITRIA
SCETIS

THMUIS
Tell el-Timai

N

Kom Aushim

KARANIS •

FAIYÛM

ARSINOE •

Medinet el-Faiyum

OXYRHYNCHUS •

El-Bahnasa

HERMOPOLIS •

El-Ashmunein

LYCOPOLIS •

Asyut

PANOPOLIS *Akhmîm*

el-Qasr wa'l-Saiyad

CHENOBOSKION

Hiw

DIOSPOLIS PARVA

TENTYRA

Dendara

HERMONTHIS • • THEBES

Armant

LATOPOLIS •

Esna

0   100 km

Scale

2   *The river Nile showing position of Pachomian monasteries in upper Egypt.*
    P. Rousseau, *Pachomius, the making of a community in fourth-century Egypt*, map 1,
    copyright University of California Press

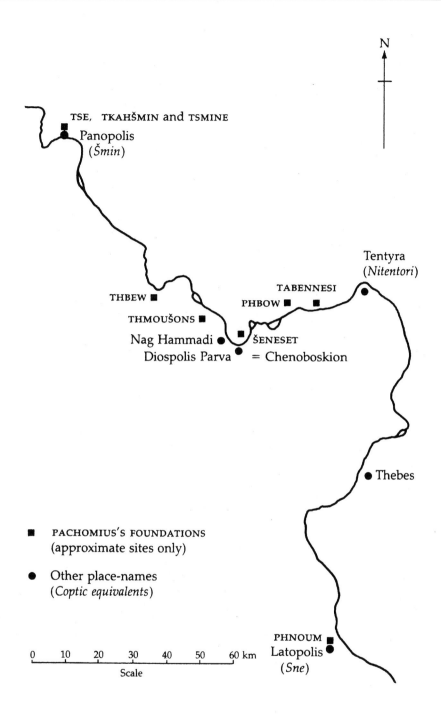

N

TSE, TKAHŠMIN and TSMINE
■
● Panopolis
(*Šmin*)

Tentyra
(*Nitentori*)

TABENNESI
THBEW ■   PHBOW ■   ■   ●
THMOUŠONS ■
Nag Hammadi ●   ■   ŠENESET
Diospolis Parva ●   = Chenoboskion

● Thebes

■ PACHOMIUS'S FOUNDATIONS
(approximate sites only)

● Other place-names
(*Coptic equivalents*)

PHNOUM ■
Latopolis ●
(*Sne*)

0   10   20   30   40   50   60 km
Scale

3   *Approximate situation of monasteries of St Pachomius in upper Egypt.*
P. Rousseau, *Pachomius . . .*, Map 2, copyright University of California Press

altered the levels reached by these (Lefort, 1939; van Elderen and Robinson, 1977; Grossmann, 1979).

Excavations at Phbow, still not fully published, have revealed three rapidly rebuilt churches, the first two brick and the third of stone. The first probably belongs to the first half of the fourth century AD, that is in the lifetime of Pachomius and the stone church, the basilica, the columns of whose arcades litter the site, to the late fourth or early fifth century. The interesting and significant point is that each rebuild was an enlargement of the previous one, the last church measuring 75m (250ft) by 35-40m (120-150ft). They were similar, plain rectangles without transepts, and divided by aisle arcades, double in the case of the last (that is four rows with a wide one in the middle). At the east end there was an apse, not projecting, but in the masonry and with two chambers on each side flanking the altar. The increasing size of the churches certainly indicates a growing number of the religious as we might well expect from written sources. No doubt the incursion of Islamic Arabs in the seventh century did little to enhance prosperity but the archaeological evidence for destruction in the eleventh century tallies with clear written sources (**4**).

It will be useful to pause and consider what had really happened in these monasteries by the river Nile. Mysticism, allowing God to enter into an individual's being, a unity with God, is essentially something that only the individual can experience, but the individual as a hermit has almost insoluble problems of food and shelter. In order to obtain the latter he has to, if not forfeit, at least sacrifice some of the ability to fulfil the former. He gives up the eremitical (hermit) life for the cenobitic or communal life, almost literally in the *koinonia*. The oppressive communality of the monastery is the very opposite of the unfettered life of the hermit. The dichotomy, the division between the two objectives runs throughout Christian, and indeed all, monasticism. The common ground is asceticism, self-inflicted discomfort or pain as proof of one's worthiness to the deity, or of course to emulate the sufferings of Christ himself. Although Pachomius was an ascetic and made himself very ill by his deprivations the extreme forms found in Syria where there was almost rivalry in this field were not found in his monasteries. The subject will come up again with Carthusians (p51).

To organise a body of men dedicated to a life of chastity confined in a small space requires fairly detailed arrangements. The Rule of Pachomius in so far as we know it from Jerome's translation, into Latin from Greek (Pachomius himself probably only spoke Coptic), was a set of precepts rather than a formal Rule like that of St Benedict. The new recruits were also largely converts and the liturgy was simple, perpetual prayer, private with formal collective prayer in the church at intervals. It owed a great deal to Jewish precedent:

> Pachomius wanted his *koinonia* to be like the primitive community of Jerusalem. The basis of this common life was fraternal charity . . . This idea of service, or even servitude, was the basis of Pachomian cenobitism (Veilloux, 1977).

No doubt the army experience of Pachomius was of great value, particularly on the need for discipline, but the picture given by Veilloux does not suggest a rigid regime, for that

4 *Phbow, plan of*
stone basilica of
c.400 AD with
earlier brick
churches below.
Peter Grossman

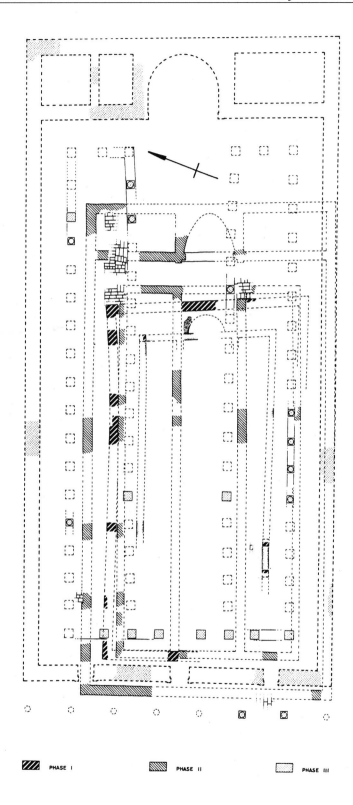

PHASE I   PHASE II   PHASE III

belongs to a much later and more sophisticated period. In the age of Pachomius miracles still happened and constant divine intervention was very apparent. There was an immediacy about early monasticism that was lost in later times.

Expansion

The monasteries of St Pachomius were not isolated in the desert, for the river Nile constituted a grand highway to Alexandria and the Mediterranean and perhaps even more importantly in the reverse direction. Perhaps the most distinguished visitor during the lifetime of Pachomius was Athanansius (296-373) (the great confounder of the Arian heresy), the archbishop of Alexandria. After the death of Pachomius the guest of most consequence was St Basil. Cassian, who spent some years in Egypt, apparently never reached the Thebaid but knew all about it and of course went to Anatolia and southern France, being greatly involved with early monasticism in both places.

Times were propitious for spreading monachism. The Roman Empire was still intact, Christianity widespread and favoured since Constantine (Adeney, 1908). The apparently Stoic element in monastic life struck a reciprocal chord in late Roman life. Over much of the Empire monasticism was well established by the end of the fourth century (**5**). In parts of Syria there was direct proselytism and the Rule of Pachomius introduced; elsewhere no doubt it was the example that had the most influence.

The spread of monasticism was in all directions: up the Nile to Ethiopia and down the Nile to the Mediterranean and then in all directions east, north and west. Nor did it stop at the boundaries of the Empire but passed beyond, particularly in the east. The great surge of Islam in the seventh century makes us forget that in the fifth and sixth centuries Christianity's main strength was in the eastern Mediterranean and north Africa where it subsequently vanished, as in north-west Africa in the Maghreb, or was greatly reduced in importance as in Egypt or the Levant and later in Anatolia. It is not necessary to describe what happened in the different regions but two areas call for mention.

Syria deserves mention because the monastic remains are perhaps the most impressive from this early period. The most famous is Qal'at Sim'an which consists of four great aisled churches or basilicas directed towards the points of the compass creating an octagonal area in the middle of which the stump of the column of St Simeon Stylites stands. It was of course higher when Simeon sat on top of it for many years, an example followed by others. This rather repugnant form of asceticism should not divert our attention from the scale of the original buildings (Braunfels, 1972, 15-19), both the churches and the mass of residential buildings attached in vaguely cloister form to south of the eastern basilica. The fifth-century aisled church is in a 'chapter house' position. Syria was very rich in the fifth and sixth centuries from the caravan trade to which Braunfels attributes this and other architecturally ambitious remains.

Celtic monasticism has a special fascination: first introduced from the Empire from which it was cut off by pagan Saxon England it was transmuted into a form suitable to Irish society. The great crosses, the round towers, the decorated manuscripts and metal work, and perhaps most important the missionary journeys of St Columba and St

Columbanus (whose severe Rule was adopted in many French monasteries), these are the features that come to mind. Very unusual was the status of bishops who held a position below abbots, quite contrary to normal medieval practice. The disappearance of buildings and perimeter enclosures means we have little knowledge of the layout of an Irish monastery. There were evidently several churches or chapels and small round buildings but no long ranges for dormitory or refectory — the building blocks of the cloister. There is an elusive oriental feeling about Irish monasticism and not just the deceptive resemblance of the round towers to minarets!

The Rule of St Benedict (*c*.480-547)

St Benedict of Nursia founded small monasteries around Subiaco in central Italy but his Rule composed at Monte Cassino, upon which his fame rests, became the basis of later *western* monasticism. It consists of 73 chapters (McCann, 1976), the reading of one each day gave the name 'Chapter House' to the place where it was read. It is not our intention to work through the Rule but one or two of the chapters are especially relevant to the subject under discussion.

The total power and authority of the abbot recalls the slightly centurion-like authority of Pachomius (chapters 2, 64, 71), for the abbot is to be regarded as the 'representative of Christ'. Obedience was one of the vows of the monk and it was to the abbot that he was to be obedient. We shall return to his duties with regard to guests (chapters 53, 56) for they had an important bearing on where he lived in the monastery discussed in this book's later chapters. The prior, the second in command, of whom we shall hear much later is to be appointed by the abbot (chapter 65), who was himself elected, not by the bishop which led to him putting on airs and undermining the abbot's authority. The relationship between a monastery and the bishop of the diocese was to be a perennial problem.

A good many of the chapters read like a 'custumal' or the timetable of what was sung or said in the seven daily offices. The backbone of the offices was the Psalms of David, a surprising reminder of how much the monks still saw themselves in continuity with the Jewish Old Testament. Modern commentators always quote with approval the prescribed manual labour and reading to be done each day (chapter 48). 'Idleness is the enemy of the soul' is an aphorism that appealed to Protestant historians.

Many of the chapters deal with daily life: food and drink in the refectory (chapters 34, 40), clothes and bedding (chapter 55) and private property (chapter 33). No private property of any kind was to be allowed: 'this vice especially ought to be utterly rooted out of the monastery'. The individual monk had no property but the institution to which he belonged could own property and in the course of years by gifts and bequests often became rich. Other chapters deal with silence (chapters 6, 42) ('as for buffoonery and talk that is vain and stirs laughter we condemn such things everywhere'), while chapter 4 gives a list of all aspects of conduct. Two chapters that especially emphasise the communal character of monastic life are 22 and 38. The weekly reader was appointed each week to read from sacred works while the meal was in progress. 'And let there be the greatest silence, so that no whisper but the reader's voice may be heard there.' Essential communication was made by sign language.

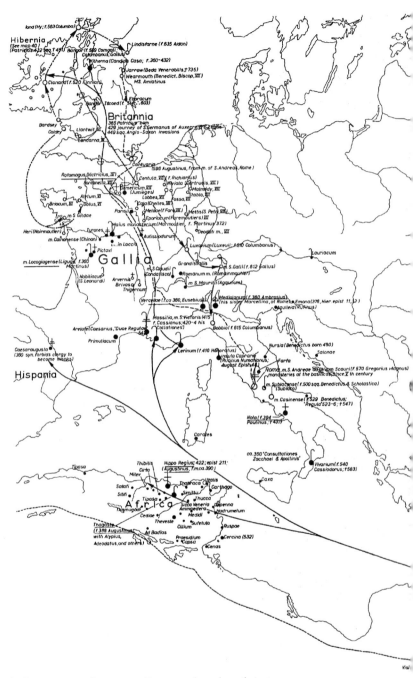

5   Map showing spread of monasticism from upper Egypt south and north in to
    Mediterranean in AD 300-700. Note reflex movement from Celtic areas.
    F. van der Meer and C. Mohrman, *Atlas of the early Christian World*, English
    edition, 1959, Nelson, plate 34

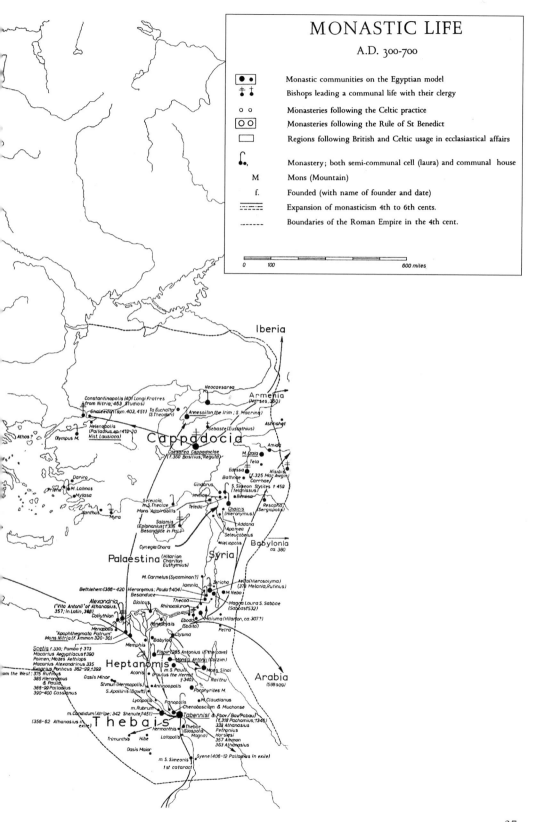

MONASTIC LIFE

A.D. 300-700

• •	Monastic communities on the Egyptian model
‡ ‡	Bishops leading a communal life with their clergy
o o	Monasteries following the Celtic practice
☐☐	Monasteries following the Rule of St Benedict
▭	Regions following British and Celtic usage in ecclasiastical affairs
✦,	Monastery; both semi-communal cell (laura) and communal house
M	Mons (Mountain)
f.	Founded (with name of founder and date)
▪▪▪▪	Expansion of monasticism 4th to 6th cents.
-------	Boundaries of the Roman Empire in the 4th cent.

0   100   600 miles

Chapter 22 was in a sense a departure from previous practice for monks in Greek Christianity and the first ones on the Nile did not sleep in a dormitory but in cells in the *laura*. St Benedict's monks slept in their clothes ready to go to quire for the first office soon after midnight. There was always to be a light in the dormitory and all the religious were to sleep together in separate beds or if this was not possible in tens or twenties, with the younger brethren mixed up with their seniors. This sleeping in a boarding-school type of dormitory or barrack room, always visible and dressed ready for the first office soon after midnight was one of the most irksome parts of monastic life and not surprisingly was abandoned in the thirteenth and fourteenth centuries. Nevertheless the need to house all the religious together in one long range was almost certainly a major factor in the creation of the cloister 300 years later.

The prior (chapter 65), the second in command, has been mentioned but two other officers (later called 'obedentiaries') deserve notice: the Dean (chapter 21) and Cellarer (chapter 31). The former's principal function was to assist the abbot, while the cellarer 'who is prudent, of mature character, temperate, not a great eater, not proud, not headstrong, not rough spoken, not lazy, not wasteful but God-fearing', had a general responsibility for maintaining goods and chattels, provisions and food. He was a sort of quartermaster and a very important figure in the monastery.

It is interesting that St Benedict in chapter 1 of the Rule says that the cenobitic monk, one living in a community under a rule, is serving a probation for the life of the hermit, the eremitical monk, 'having learnt in association with many brethren how to fight against the devil'. In other words the Rule allowed the monk to prepare himself for the higher form of monasticism, as a hermit, a return to the desert as it were. While it is difficult to believe that many Benedictines returned to the life of the solitary it is interesting as demonstrating the continued belief in the superiority of the eremitical as opposed to the cenobitic life for a contemplative, the freedom of the desert over monastic enclosure.

English monasticism before the Vikings

Between the dispatch in 596 of St Augustine of Canterbury by Pope Gregory I (Gregory the Great) and the incursion of the Vikings from *c*.800 that put an end to all or nearly all of the English monasteries there was a flourishing period of English monasticism, noted particularly for its missionary work on the Continent. Gregory himself was a monk and it is especially significant that it was monks who were charged with converting the heathen English and monks in their turn that went to convert heathen peoples on the Continent.

Although a number of interesting churches survive, some of which were monastic, very little is known about the monastic building associated with them. Pope Gregory (540-604), a great reformer of the papacy and author of a life of St Benedict, might have been expected to insist on the promulgation of the Rule but there is no evidence for this. What is reasonably clear is that the cloister *sensu stricto* was quite unknown.

At Abingdon abbey, Berkshire, we have a description of the earliest monastic church built by Abbot Heane in 675: 120ft (35m) long with apses at both ends and 12 habitations with chapels set radially around them (Stevenson, ii, 272). Clearly there was no cloister

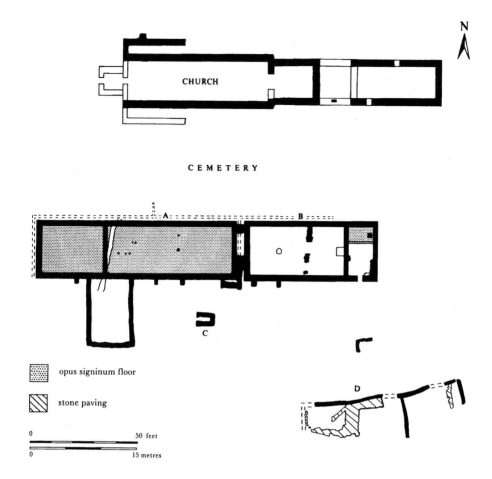

6   Jarrow, plan of excavated range of seventh-/eighth-century monastery. R. Cramp

and the inspiration seems to be a Celtic monastery. The site was surrounded by a high wall. It was replaced in the tenth century by a church modelled on the Cluniac house at Fleury in France.

At Whitby on the Yorkshire coast excavations yielded a very rich haul of Middle Saxon finds on the north side of the later church (Peers and Radford, 1943) but structures, small rectangular buildings, were less clear than the confirming datable material.

The most informative excavations have been in Northumbria at the monastery associated with the Venerable Bede (673-735), Jarrow in County Durham (Cramp 1969). A quite sophisticated rectangular building lay parallel to the churches separated from them by a cemetery (**6**). There was no enclosure, no cloister, but by analogy with later cloisters it has been identified as a refectory. It seems clear that Bede did not write his *Ecclesiastical History* in a cloister as we understand the term. It can also be inferred that English missionaries of the eight century like Boniface (*c*.680-754) took no knowledge of the cloister with them to the Continent.

It seems clear that the cloister *sensu stricto* was unknown in England in the seventh and eighth centuries. Nevertheless if Jarrow is compared with what we know of Irish monasteries of this period, at the former there is potential for a cloister in the ranges, while in the latter the differences clearly go far beyond the form of tonsure or date of Easter, to a very different concept of a monastery (Workman, 1913). Irish monks played no part in the creation of the cloister.

2 The origin and development
of the cloister

The origin and development
of the cloister

The central issue in the discussion of the origin of the cloister is whether it was hit upon by trial and error or whether it was deliberately designed; much of the discussion since the nineteenth century has been prompted by the famous ninth-century plan in the cathedral library of St Gall, Switzerland. Before turning to that plan it may be wise to look at the principal elements in what we call the *cloister.*

The word is sometimes used on the Continent to apply to the whole monastic enclosure or the wall surrounding it, a feature of virtually all monasteries. Thus the Germans speak of a *Kloster* (the monastery) and use the word *Klaisur* for what we in English would call the cloister. It is important to recognise the distinction which otherwise can lead to confusion.

For the English speaker the cloister is an area, usually square and always rectangular, enclosed on three sides and attached to the monastic church on the fourth. It may lie on either the north or south side of the nave, the western arm of the church. In very exceptional cases like Rochester cathedral it may be attached to the eastern arm. The four sides of this courtyard are now discussed starting with the church.

On the cloister side ground-floor windows had to be suppressed in the cloister alley and the church wall pierced for doorways giving access to the cloister, but otherwise the church did not need any alteration. The essential element was that the nave was long enough for a square to be formed on it. In the recent excavations at the Cistercian abbey of Fountains in Yorkshire it was demonstrated that when the tiny early church was to be replaced by the present one the cloister had been laid out first (*see* **19**), the length of the western arm of the church being to some degree determined by the position of the west range of the cloister (Gilyard-Beer and Coppack, 1986). This very neatly illustrates the close relationship between the length of the nave and the size of the cloister square or garth. Reference has already been made to the shortness of many eastern churches compared to western ones epitomised in the great nave of Emperor Constantine's church of Old St Peter's at Rome (now demolished) and the shortness of Emperor Justinian's church of St Sophia at Istanbul.

From the earliest times of monasticism eating had been a communal activity and the solemn form in which the Benedictine Rule required it to be done needed a long building with tables arranged in such a way that the reader's voice could be heard throughout above the sound of utensils being used. Its position was influenced by the kitchen which served it and was one of the most disturbing elements in a monastery; the refectory need to be furthest from the church with the kitchen beyond it (cf. **7**). This was the normal position

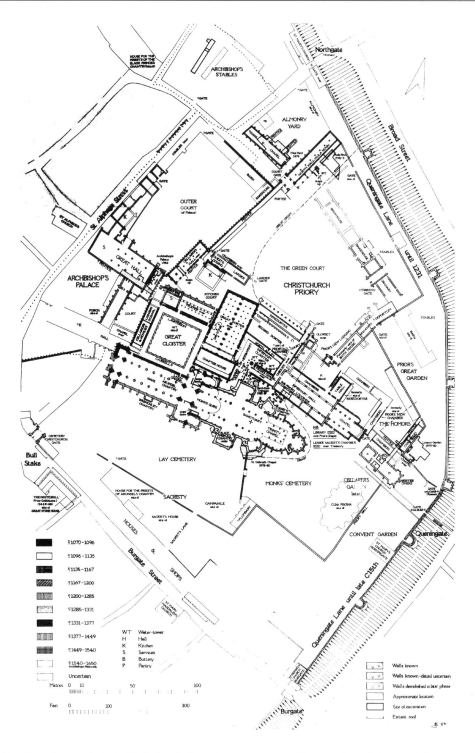

7 *Canterbury cathedral, Christchurch Benedictine monastery Note northern cloister with huge
dormitory and large aisled infirmary to east.* Canterbury Archaeological Trust

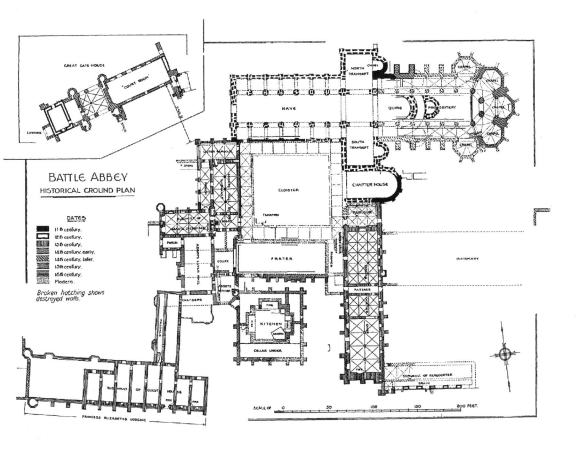

8   *Battle, Sussex, Benedictine abbey. Dated plan. South cloister. Note the development in west range for the abbot's lodging.* H. Brakspear, *Archaeologia*, 83

in a Benedictine monastery although the kitchen was brought forward to the cloister by the Cistercians as we shall see later (p55).

Communal sleeping required by the Benedictine Rule (see p28) could only be satisfactorily housed in a long roofable building and preferably out of view of the cloister on the first floor. As the first office was sung soon after midnight, close proximity to the quire where it took place was desirable so the monks could proceed straight to it from their beds. The most convenient place evidently was to set it at right angles as an extension of the south transept (or north transept in a north cloister) with access to the quire. At first this was along the cloister alley but later it was by a staircase at the south end of the transept — 'the night stairs' (cf. **8**).

To close the courtyard a third range was required on the west side and to some degree a function had to be invented for it. It was usually vaulted over the ground floor like the secular domestic hall from which it was likely to have been derived, and as with that building the ground floor or part of it was used as a cellar or for storage. The upper floor

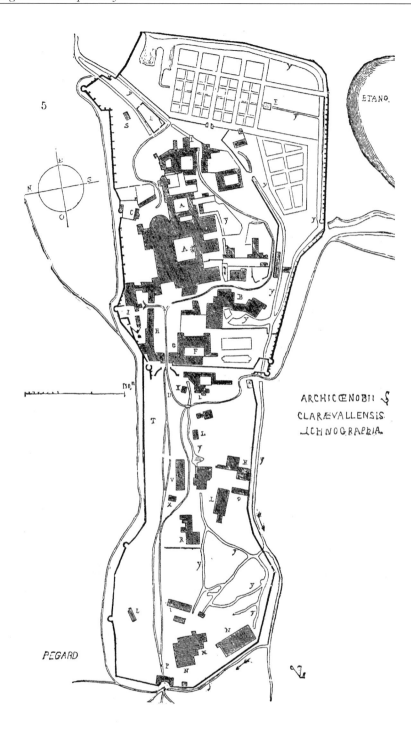

9   *Clairvaux. An eighteenth-century plan of the abbey and ancillary buildings: church and cloister (A), abbot's and guest's house (GF), St Bernard's cell (C), the fish ponds (E), the main gate (P), and other service buildings. Compare the St Gall plan in* **11**. Viollet-le-Duc

could be used as guest hall, abbot's hall and chamber (Benedictine), dormitory for lay brethren with their refectory below (Cistercian), and in the drawings of the monasteries in late seventeenth-century France it could be a granary, library, or infirmary; its function was clearly an unstable one. As its primary function had been to fill the open side of the cloister usually facing the external main gate of the monastery it was the natural place for entry to the cloister through an 'outer parlour' at the north end acting as a sort of filter where monks met outsiders. The west range might be dispensed with altogether as at Westminster Abbey where it was demolished and a new house built for the abbot in the fourteenth century.

We now have a four-sided courtyard but to convert this into a cloister the four alleys or walks, roofed over, have to be introduced set against the church and ranges on the outside and with an open area or *garth* in the middle. This could be storeyed with arcades at both levels, in the Mediterranean area at all events. The feeling is quite unlike a Classical peristyle where the columns are essentially ornamental since the purpose was to form an enclosed space lit by a window arcade where the monks could read and write as if it were indoors. The window openings were indeed glazed in the later Middle Ages. The garth was ornamental with a lawn or flowers in it and it was never used for burial except by the Carthusians (p48) with their rather gloomier outlook. A circular fountain or wash-place (*lavabo*) might be constructed against the south alley for washing before entering the refectory but in English monasteries this was usually replaced by a trough in the south wall of the alley (**10**).

10 Fountains Abbey. Lavabo trough in the south alley of cloister flanking the central door to the refectory which is at right angles to the alley. NMR, Crown Copyright

A little cloister could be added on the east side of the east range containing the infirmary or sick bay in medieval times and in post-medieval Continental houses a multiplicity of 'cloisters' with Classical arcades might be added. These have little resemblance to the medieval cloister.

The elements of the cloister have been discussed but when and where were they put together to create one? It was unlikely that a need was felt for such an arrangement before the Rule of St Benedict was fully adopted, and that was some two centuries after his death. Cloisters have been claimed from the eighth century or even the seventh century at Jumieges (Jacobsen, 1992, 19-43). That there was a fumbling towards such a formation is inherently likely, as has been suggested at Jarrow (p30). It is unlikely that it would have been successful or widely adopted until there was some agency seeking to impose uniformity over a large area on the one hand and an agent on the other to carry it out. The Carolingian empire, especially under the successor of Charlemagne, Louis the Pious (814-40), could have been the former and the abbey of Cluny (founded 910) the second.

The St Gall plan

St Gall started life as an Irish hermit's place of settlement in north-east Switzerland in the seventh century but grew into a Benedictine monastery of importance. It was secularised in Napoleonic times and in due course became a cathedral which still retains a very rich collection of medieval manuscripts housed in the former abbot's house. Among the manuscripts is a parchment measuring 112cm by 77cm (3ft 9in by 2ft 6in) formed by five pieces of parchment stitched together (Jacobsen, 1992). On the reverse side is a *Life of St Martin of Tours*, and on the other the famous early ninth-century plan, ruled out in red ink, with which we are concerned here (**11**).

It bears a long inscription on the east side by the cemetery on the plan explaining that it had been given to 'my sweetest son' (*dulcissime fili*) Gozbert by an unnamed donor as a:

> briefly annotated copy of the layout of the monastic building with which you may exercise your ingenuity and recognise my devotion whereby I trust you do not find me slow to satisfy your wishes. Do not imagine that I have undertaken this task supposing you to stand in need of our instruction but rather believe that our love of God and in the friendly zeal of brotherhood I have depicted this for you alone to scrutinize. Farewell in Christ, always mindful of us. Amen.
> (Translation in Horn and Born, 1979, i, 10)

It can be confidently assumed that this was addressed to Gozbert, abbot of St Gall abbey 816-36 who in 820 started his rebuilding of the monastery to which the donor refers. The identity of the donor is not known although presumably a senior monk, possibly moving in high, if not imperial, circles. The church itself, the present cathedral, has been rebuilt in the late medieval times and the eighteenth century, but Jacobsen has been able to demonstrate from some enigmatic figures on the plan that it was to some degree used in the arcades (Jacobsen, 1992). The plan is not a specific building plan but a fairly detailed design of an entire monastery to give guidance and suggestions to someone who was intending to build one. Its value is therefore incalculable on contemporary views about laying out such a group of buildings, bearing in mind its theoretical but not utopian character. It was almost certainly never built in the form we see. The pinholes in the fabric indicated to Jacobsen that it was an original design, not a copy or tracing. The astonishing feature from the historians' point of view is its close correspondence with medieval abbey plans of the following centuries suggesting it or close copies were taken as an example to follow by building abbots (**11**).

To orientate the reader the long building in the middle with round ends (apses) is the church running east-west with altars at both ends. Many buildings are disposed all around it. The square structure lying to the south is the cloister enclosure. Around this central group on the periphery are a whole series of square buildings, which are thought to have been timber-framed; the church and cloister buildings were intended to be built in stone. All the buildings are very carefully labelled in ninth-century Latin so there is no problem of identification. The literature on the plan from the nineteenth and twentieth centuries, mainly in German, is enormous (Jacobsen, 1992, bibliography), but an article by the great Victorian architectural historian, Robert Willis (1848), and the great three-volume work by Horn and Born (1979) with many conjectural reconstructions provides the English reader with ample material on the subject.

To return to the plan: entry to the monastic enclosure was by a gate on the west. The building on the left bearing a later inscription is of uncertain purpose while the six rectangles on the right are animal pens. The two concentric circles loosely attached to the church are free-standing towers at its west end. Entry to the church was by the 'Western Paradise', a semi-circular partly-roofed enclosure at the west end of the church, a sort of forecourt, its inner part open to the sky. A door on the left led into the church. The western altar was on the right and columns are shown forming the arcades for the nave by their square bases. In each bay, the transverse divisions, there were chapels with altars with their dedications recorded. The eastern altar was the more important and had a crypt beneath it. The east end terminated in the 'Eastern Paradise', a sort of forecourt open to the sky; 'without roof' is specifically mentioned. The plan has no scale but the estimates from presumed units used would make the church over 100m long. The question of dimensions and many other matters relating to the church need not concern us since our subject is the cloister. It is worth remarking that double-ended churches of this kind are not unknown elsewhere in the region, notably a third stage of construction at Cologne, but St Gall appears to be the earliest.

The three ranges of the cloister are shown with great clarity, each labelled and its functions depicted. All three were two-storeyed: the east range at first-floor level with arrangement of beds (77) shown in the dormitory down the centre and against the wall while below it the warming room is recorded; the south range with refectory at ground-floor level with a longitudinal arrangement of tables with abbot's and guests' seating and vestments in the loft above; the west range with barrels for beer and wine below and the larder on the first floor (**12 & 13**). The dormitory had an attached latrine and bathhouse at its south end. The refectory had a square kitchen with cooking stove in the middle

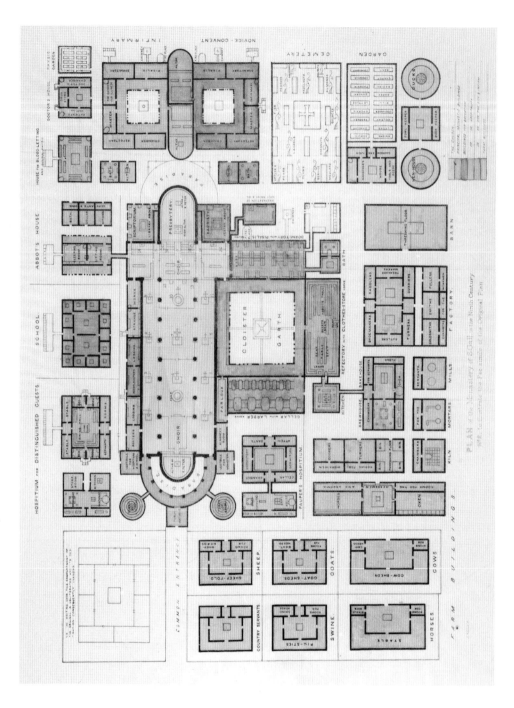

11a St Gall plan, showing classification of buildings by Robert Willis in 1848

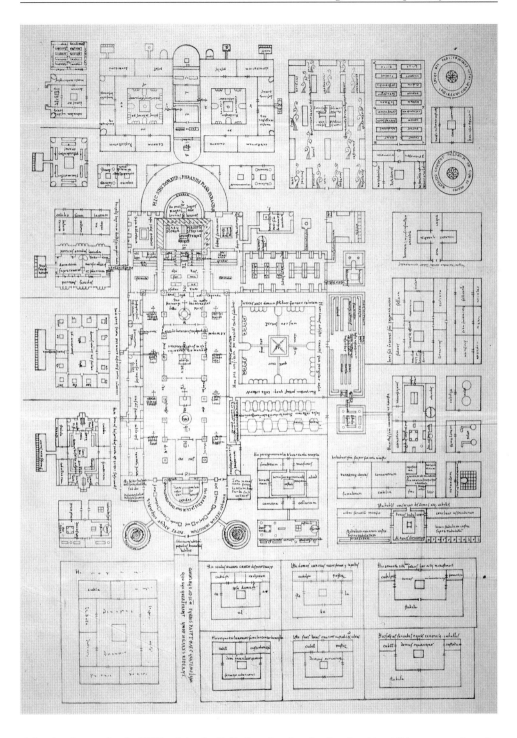

11b Another version by Willis of the St Gall plan showing the church with additions on north and south including abbot's house on north transept and cloister on south transept

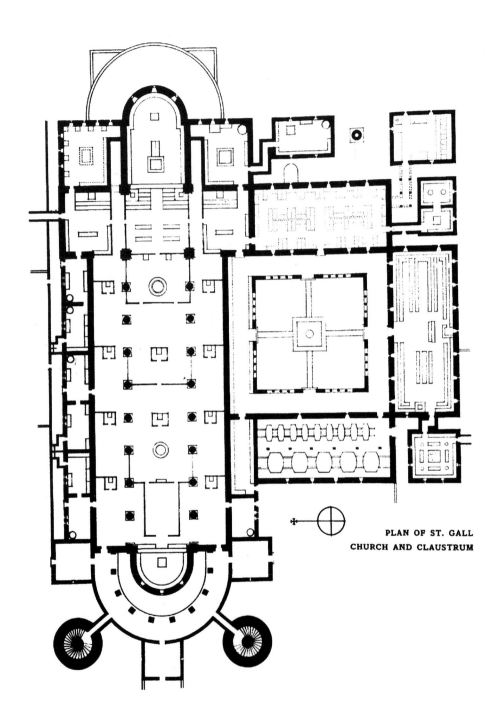

PLAN OF ST. GALL
CHURCH AND CLAUSTRUM

*12 St Gall Plan: Church and cloister as interpreted by Horn and Born to show the intended buildings.
The plan of St Gall, 1979, Berkeley, vol.1 fig. 107, photographed by Robert P. Dittmer*

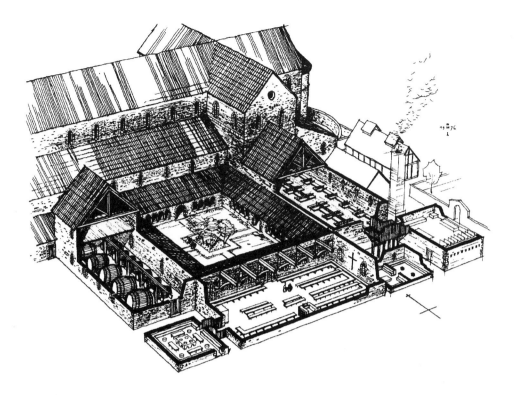

13 *St Gall Plan: cutaway elevations of conjectural reconstruction of cloister ranges by Horn and Born. Note detailed furniture from original in dormitory, refectory and west ranges. The first floor has been omitted from the last two. Plan of St Gall*, 1979, Berkeley, vol 1, fig. 192, Photographed by Robert P. Ditttmer

linked by an angled passage to its west end. The kitchen itself was linked on the south by a passage to the bakehouse and brewhouse. There was outside access to the cloister through an outer parlour in its north-west corner. A door led from the south transept to the eastern alley while the dormitory seems to have had its own access into the transept. One of the difficulties of the plan is that steps and staircases are not shown.

Four spacious alleys enclose the garth reached by four doorways at points of the compass in the centre of each side, flanked by pairs of arched openings looking into the garth. Paths from the doorways lead to a square central area in the garth upon which are four boughs of juniper (*Savina*) directed towards the corners. Possibly they are not symbolic but had a scent that was regarded as hygienic or medicinal.

For anyone who wished to study the medieval cloister there could hardly be a better point to start than with this idealised, rather graph-paper drawing with its detailed labelling. The main absentee is the chapter house, not specifically mentioned in the Rule, but an essential element from the tenth/eleventh century onwards. It was the place for the daily reading of a chapter of the Rule after morning mass but where much other business such as confessions, punishments and so on took place. It was set on the ground floor by the south end of the transept beneath the dormitory, at right angles to the eastern alley and often had a decorated doorway flanked by decorated windows. It projected beyond the range and caused problems about carrying the dormitory over its vault. In the St Gall plan the warming room would have had to be moved to make room for it. Its functions were perhaps to be performed in the north alley at St Gall where the inscription reads: *Hinc pia consilium pertractet turba salubre* (whence confusion of faith may undergo healthy advice).

The number of latrine seats at the south end of the dormitory seems small in relation to the number of beds in it. Real later refectories may be on the first floor but a vestiary in the loft over them has no parallels. The most incongruous feature of the cloister is the whole of the west range being devoted to drink on the ground floor and larder above. While St Benedict allowed some wine, such a large building devoted to this and the larder seems quite inappropriate in this position for a body devoted to abstention. One has a feeling that the range is still in an experimental stage with regard to use.

The whole monastery was conceived of as a great group of farm and estate buildings with church and convent replacing the secular mansion. The buildings may be mentioned (all timber-framed according to Horn and Born): to the south-west animal pens for sheep, pigs, goats and cows and accommodation for those tending them; to the south workshops, brewhouse, bakehouse, granary and stables; to the east were enclosures for hens and geese (on the south), vegetable garden, main cemetery in an orchard, the infirmary complex comprising two blocks for infirmary and novices with the house for physicians at its north end, with the misericord or house for blood-letting (a medical function). On the north side of the church lay the abbot's house (*mansio abbatis*) with its own kitchen, bathhouse and latrines, a school and an elaborate guesthouse for distinguished visitors with its own brewhouse, bakehouse and kitchen. The school to the north was probably for oblate children, dedicated by their parents to become monks. The curious rake-like projections from these buildings and those on the east are evidently latrines with seats discharging into a drain running round the perimeter. Down the side of the church from the east were scriptorium below and library above, lodging for visiting monks, the schoolmaster's and porter's lodging and the entry for the distinguished visitors into the church. South of the crypt in the church was a two-storeyed building with the sacristy below and vestry above.

Most of the buildings mentioned would be found in any large rural monastery of the high Middle Ages, even the farmyard part. Evidently part of the intention for the creation of the cloister was to separate out the residence of the religious from the mundane world, particularly on the south and the west. This was probably little different from the position on a large lay estate. The north side of the church was especially favoured and hidden of course by the church from the south. The abbot's house deserves special attention, as the abbot is the subject of our next chapter.

The *mansic abbatis* was an imposing two-storeyed building with its own latrines to the north and kitchen and baths to the east (**14**). The Rule (chapter 56) instructed the abbot to 'eat always with guests and pilgrims'; this house may also have functioned as a guesthouse to judge by the number of beds shown in it. It was divided at both levels into two rooms (dormitory and hall below, chamber and solar above) which were heated and clearly provided ample accommodation. It had not the remotest resemblance to the English ground-floor hall, except that the verandahs on either side resemble aisles.

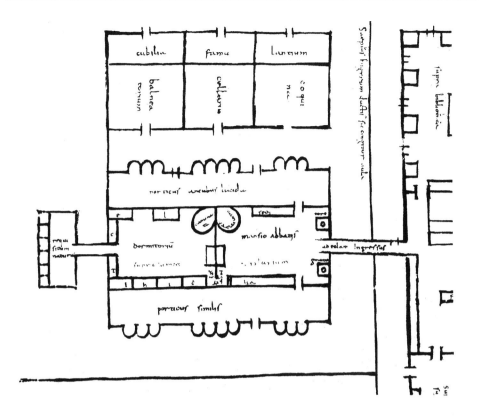

*14 St Gall Plan: the abbot's house (*mansio). *Note passage from north side of church, verandahs, latrines, bathhouse, storeroom and kitchen. The house is divided centrally at each level with chamber and solarium on first floor. Note fireplaces or stoves.* Horn and Born, *Plan of St Gall*, 1979, vol. 1 fig. 251, photographed from colour print verso to remove MS discoloration by Robert P. Dittmer. Copyright MS Stiftsbibliotek St Gallen. Cod. Sang 1092

The placing of the abbot's residence on the north side of the church, far away from the religious in the cloister on the south, raises some questions. Among the edicts following the synods of Aachen in 816 and 817 issued by Louis the Pious (Braunfels, 1972, 234-6) the abbot could only feed guests in the refectory where he had to feed himself. A later edict authorised the abbot to have a cell with the monks or canons, not less than six monks living together which is a roundabout way of saying that the abbot should sleep in the dormitory. Although the abbot had a table (*mensa abbatis*) in the refectory it is fairly clear that the designer of the St Gall plan expected him to live in a substantial house on the other side of the church. Whether this was normal practice at the time it is hard to say. It is difficult to believe that the great Carolingian monastic reformer, St Benedict of Aniane (not the author of the Rule), approved of such an arrangement, even if the plan was made by someone sharing the views of the second St Benedict on reform. It may be added that one of the principal objects of the reformers was to see that the Rule was strictly enforced in all houses, a fair indication that this had not yet happened.

With regard to the question of the origin of the cloister posed at the beginning of this chapter, whether it was stumbled upon more or less accidentally or designed deliberately we can say that there was probably element of both. The idea of a residential courtyard attached to the nave of the church may have arisen in the eastern part of the Carolingian Empire but was only formalised in a complete form in the time of Louis the Pious. The earlier monastic plans at Lorsch (Hessen) or St Riquier (Somme) are sufficiently close to later orthodoxy not to be ignored and seventh-century Jumieges was clearly pointing in the right direction. The St Gall plan itself still has an experimental element even if it is so mature in many ways. If it merely corresponded with current practice why offer it to Abbot Gozbert in *c*.820 for consideration? Clearly there was an innovative, not to say theoretical, element in it even if its designer was very familiar with current practice. We can learn much from it.

Modification of the cloister in response to reforming Orders

If the cloister had reached a stable form by the ninth and tenth centuries the agent that spread it over much of Europe was the great abbey of Cluny in Burgundy. Founded in 910 under a remarkable series of abbots, both the church and its ancillary buildings grew to enormous size and European influence by the mid-twelfth century. Sadly, except for one transept, the church and most of the ancillary buildings were destroyed in Napoleonic times. The reconstructions of the church on an ever-increasing scale have given rise to the titles Cluny I, II and III, although the changes in the ancillary buildings do not coincide with the church reconstructions (Conant, 1968). Cluny I was destroyed by its successors but we have a fairly clear idea of the nature of the cloister, as indeed for the whole layout for Cluny II and III as shown in **15**, of Cluny in 1088. The outline of the vast Cluny III on the left gives some idea of the relative scale. The interesting point is that the cloister seems to have already outgrown the church, extending beyond the transept in the east end and beyond the 'galilee' (western entry) and atrium in the west. One feels indeed that the growth of the cloister with its huge refectory, was the driving requirement for the vast new church with its splendid *chevet* of radial apses.

The end of the eleventh and most of the twelfth century saw the Hildebrandine reforms (Pope Gregory VII, 1073-85), the first crusade, the struggle of pope and emperor, the twelfth-century renaissance and so on; everything conspired to give superiority to the church. It was against this background that the great monastic reformers set to work, starting as breakaways from Benedictine monasteries. There were six main foundations of new Orders, as they are now called, taking their names from the place of the first foundation: Carthusian (Chartreusce), Cistercian (Citeaux), Savigniac (Savigny), Grandmontine (Grandmont), Fontevrault and Tiron. It was the first two, the most important, that will be discussed here, whose influence on the form of cloister was profound. Before doing this mention must be made of another two groups: the canons regular who lived by a rule and were monks in all but name.

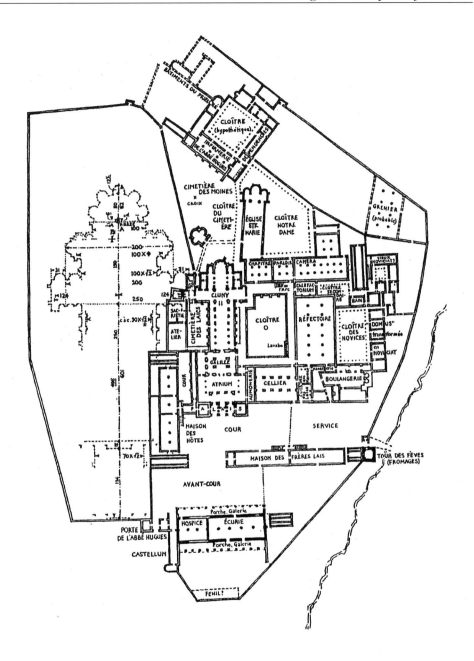

15 *Cluny ii, the abbey in 1088. Note enlarged cloister on south side of church seeming to fit better on the final enlarged church show in outline to north. K. Conant, Cluny, les eglises . . . 1968, groupe 1 planche 5, fig. 5, Medieval Academy of America*

Canons Regular

St Augustine (354-430), Bishop of Hippo (in Algeria), author of the *City of God*, had admired St Anthony and the desert hermits but never himself became a monk. However, towards the end of his life he did live a kind of collegiate life with his household and it was upon this way of life that the Augustinian Rule was based. This was the Rule adopted by the Black and White canons (the name referring to the colour of their habit), Augustinians and Premonstratensians (from Prémontré in France). The details of the Rule need not concern us here except to say that their priestly origins were reflected in their being largely ordained priests, at least in the case of the Augustinians. For a nobleman who wished to found a new religious house that could also provide priests to conduct services in his numerous chapels this was an important consideration. Foundations for Black canons therefore proliferated in the early twelfth century, particularly in the reign of Henry I (1100-35), while foundations for White canons were later in the middle of the twelfth century. What was the difference between them?

The Augustinians like the Benedictines were independent with houses not responsible to any overall authority while the White canons modelling themselves on the Cistercians not only adopted the colour of their habit but recognised a central authority and held annual assemblies (chapters). Like the latter they were a stricter order with a higher degree of asceticism. They did not adopt the Cistercian style of architecture and the cloisters for both orders of canons do not differ significantly from the Benedictine except in some differences in the refectory and chapter house — for example the former may be two-storeyed. The remains of canons' houses are amongst the most common in the English countryside but they were not great innovators, architecturally content to accept the Benedictine forms already in use.

Carthusians

St Bruno of Cologne (*c.*1030-1101) founded the monastery of the Grand Chartreuse near Grenoble in France from where the Order spread in small numbers over France and arrived later in England. The Carthusians ignored much of the Rule of St Benedict or even that of St Pachomius, wishing to return to the desert so to speak, although obviously not all the changes of cenobitic life could be discarded.

In a way Carthusians were in revolt against the dormitory, against all those elements of communality that are the very basis of the Benedictine Rule: sleeping, latrines, eating, everyone together the whole 24 hours except for individual work or writing. The Benedictine could escape the communality of the monastery by work, especially in writing the histories and chronicles upon which we depend for our knowledge of the period. Then the monk was his own individual master. The Carthusians adopted a much more radical solution.

The layout of a Carthusian monastery was the reverse of that of a normal Benedictine one in that the inner or great cloister dominated the plan and the outer or great court with the support services of a Benedictine monastery became a rather small attachment (**16, 17**) with the entry to the monastery, guesthouse and service buildings. The great cloister had a small church on one side, normally the south, together with a small refectory and chapter house all dominated by the three sides of the great cloister. This had small alleys or pentice

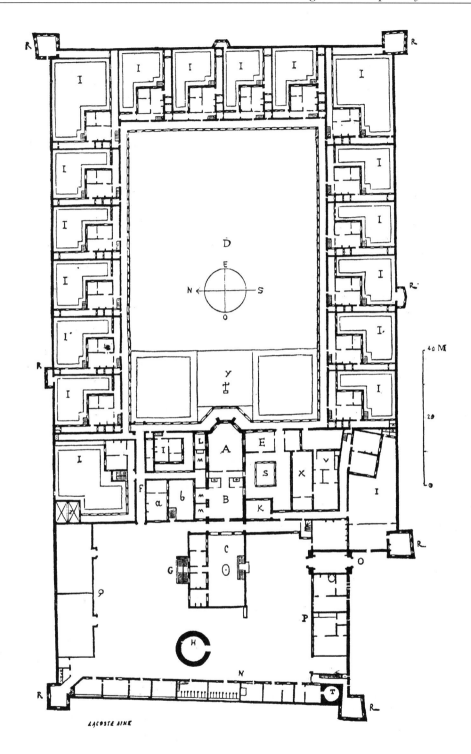

16 Clermont, Puy-de-Dome. Carthusian monastery. Note cells (I) in great Cloister (D), church (A), chapter house (E), refectory (X), cemetery (Y), prison (Z). Viollet-le-Duc

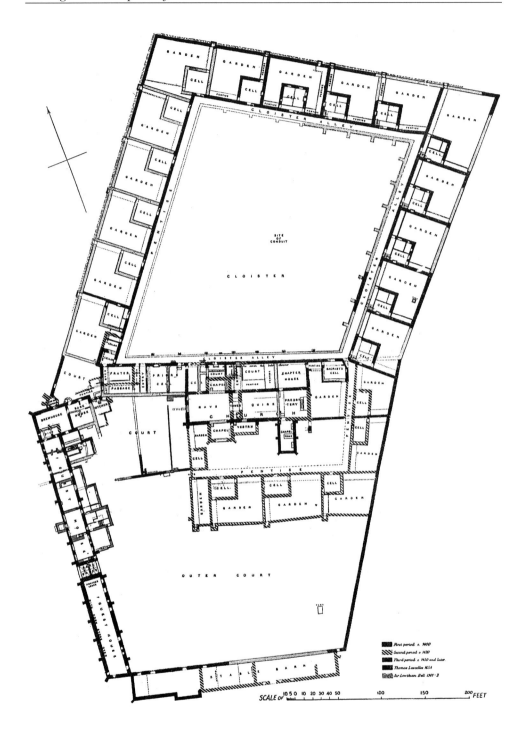

17 *Mount Grace priory, Yorkshire. Carthusian monastery: Great Cloister with cells, church and chapter house on south, guest house in outer court.* W. St J. Hope, *Yorkshire Archaeological Journal* 18

passages on four sides from which the doorways opened into the individual cells of each monk. Each cell, almost like a small cottage, was set in a small garden (**18**). The enclosure was set against common walls back and front and a path from the cell led to a latrine against the outer wall discharging into a drain that ran round the periphery of the site. Meals were taken in the refectory only on special feast days so each cell was furnished with an angled hatch so that the monk and the deliverer of food did not see each other. In the cell, besides a bed, there was the necessary furniture required for study and prayer.

The Carthusian monk was not immured in his cell for he came out for night vigils and offices and presumably attending chapter. It should be remarked that many of the chapters in the Benedictine Rule were irrelevant to this way of life. There was apparently no infirmary or misericord for blood-letting (place with a social connotation in Benedictine life) and medical attention was evidently given in the cell. While with other Orders the monks' cemetery was out of sight to the north or east of the church for Carthusians the monks were buried in the garth, the graves being seen daily. Normally for a monk death was a matter for rejoicing, a summons to the duty to which his life had been dedicated, but for the Carthusian this was taken literally, the graves being a reminder of the joys to come.

So the Carthusian's life was not totally isolated, not as in the desert for even in his cell he no doubt could hear coughing or snoring from adjoining cells as a reminder of the community around him; he was in no sense a hermit. He could do manual work in the cell or cultivate the garden that is if he had such an aptitude. The main object of the unusual claustral arrangements was solitary devotion in his oratory, but the gregarious nature of most of us would make such a life difficult to bear. Limited recruitment always kept down the number of houses in this Order, so its drastic remodelling of the cloister was never a threat to the orthodox design of the larger orders.

Nevertheless the steps taken by the Carthusians to alter the accepted arrangements underline the inherent problems of those closely following the Rule with its oppressive communality. That the Carthusians were thinking along the right lines is suggested by the famous aphorism applied to them '*Numquam reformata quia numquam deformata*', never reformed because never deformed, i.e. never needing to be reformed. Unlike the other Orders where constant backsliding had to be periodically corrected the rigidity of their life hardly allowed room for lapses. The steadfastness of the Carthusians had a terrible ending at the Reformation when refusing to accept the Act of Supremacy a number paid with their lives on the scaffold.

Cistercians

The creation of the Cistercian Order (the White monks because of their habit), the figure of St Bernard, abbot of Clairvaux in Burgundy, dominated the middle years of the twelfth century (**9, 20**). So great was the enthusiasm at the time that foundations spread over the whole of Europe and into the Holy Land and a halt had to be called to the creation of new houses. In England monastic studies have tended to be dominated by the great Cistercian ruins of Yorkshire. The secession of the Benedictine monks from St Mary's, York, and their sufferings before creating the great Cistercian abbey of Fountains is a household story (Gilyard-Beer & Coppack, 1986). We can recapture some of the enthusiasm of the time in Walter Daniel's *Life of Ailred* (Powicke, 1950). Coming down

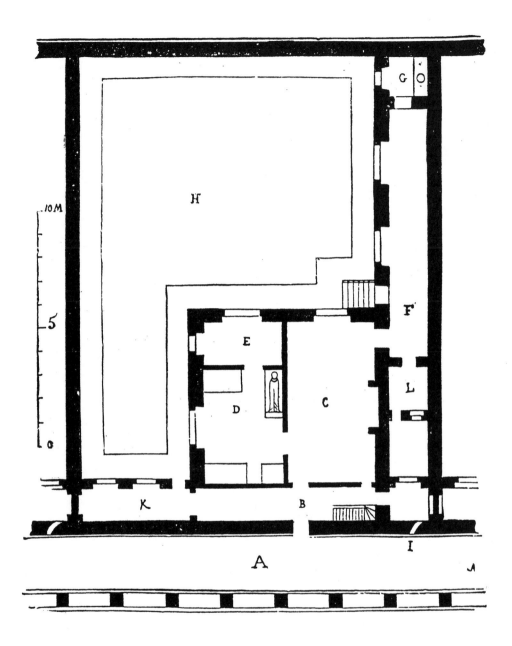

18 Clermont (**16**), a cell and garden from great cloister: alley of cloister (A), second passage isolating
cell (B), window in to garden (K), a heated room (C), cell with bed, bench and bookshelves and
oratory (E), corridor to latrine (FG), the garden (H), hatch for food on top of tower (I).
Viollet-le-Duc

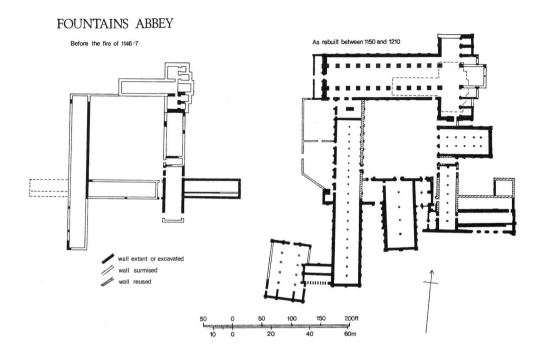

FOUNTAINS ABBEY

Before the fire of 1146-7

As rebuilt between 1150 and 1210

wall extant or excavated
wall surmised
wall reused

50   0   50   100   150   200ft
10   0   20   40   60m

19 Fountains Abbey, Yorkshire. Cistercian. Note construction of large cloister preceded the erection of the present church. Gilyard Beer & Coppack, *Archaeologia*, 108

from Scotland Ailred heard that 'certain monks had come to England from across the sea'. This refers to Rievaulx just founded from St Bernard's Clairvaux. Ailred joined the 'second paradise' and later became abbot of its daughter house at Revesby, Lincolnshire and in due course abbot of Rievaulx itself. Unlike the passivity of the Carthusians it was the restless activity of the Cistercians with their confidence in founding and building that caused such enthusiasm.

How did they differ from the Benedictines and with what consequences for the cloister? As their professed purpose in the *Carta Caritatis* was the much stricter application of the Rule of the blessed Benedict was it merely a question of degree? In a sense it was, but as with most reforms it was dissatisfaction with existing practice, particularly of Cluniacs, that largely motivated them: the elaborate liturgy, the profusely decorated buildings. Simplicity was the answer in the architecture and this indeed impresses us wherever we meet Cistercian architecture whether it be in its home territory of France or in Italy or Portugal. After the exuberance of the Romanesque the chaste and modest forms of a Cistercian church are very pleasing.

The richness of decoration and liturgy in a Cluniac abbey rested on the solid wealth of great property holdings from gift and bequest, on endowments of numerous manors from which flowed rents and labour services. The Cistercians seem to have recoiled, at least in

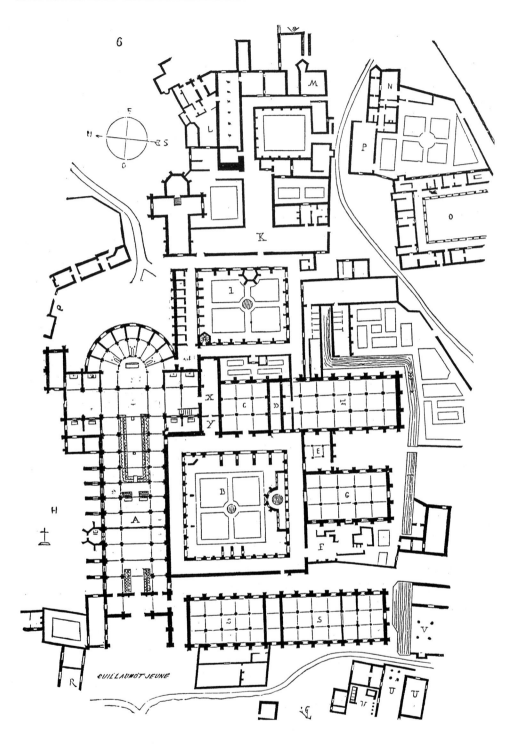

20 Clairvaux, Church (A), cloister (B), chapter house (C), warming room (E), refectory (G),
    kitchen (F), little cloister (I), former abbot's house (N), and his hall (P) etc. Viollet-le-Duc

the early years, from being merely a rentier body; by using its own labour to farm directly and so producing its own income. Surely one came nearer to what St Benedict had in mind for an ideal abbey even if the saint had been silent on how a monastery should support itself. So instead of manors they had 'granges' that is farms worked directly by the house itself (Platt, 1969). The monks could not work these with their own hands and large numbers of lay-brethren (*conversi*) were employed in agriculture. Those who lived in the monastery used the nave of the church for their services, since although they had taken the normal vows, they were not regarded as quire monks. They slept on the first floor of the west range and had part of the ground floor as their refectory. In larger monasteries they had their own infirmary and latrines.

The consequences of introducing such a large number of new men into the cloister were considerable. The abbot could no longer have his quarters in the first floor of the west range and was banished to the east range (p67). There were far more mouths to feed and attempts to retain the refectory in its original position parallel to the south alley proved unsatisfactory so it was swung through a right angle to finish like the chapter house at right angles to the cloister alley. This created voids on either side which could be filled by a kitchen with serving hatches for both monks and lay brothers on one side and the warming room on the other (**21, 22**). Other changes created by pressure on space were the lengthening of east and west ranges, particularly the latter to reproduce the remarkable west range at Fountains. In medieval times the surviving vaulted ground floor would have been subdivided but the first-floor dormitory would have given a spectacular vista. In the east range the night stairs leading down to the transept and quire became a very definite feature, which in Benedictine dormitories had hardly existed.

The changes must not be exaggerated for the Benedictine cloister remained essentially intact architecturally even if the functions altered in some of the ranges. There was perhaps a greater contrast between the eastern and western sides, the real monks on the east range being more cut off than formerly from activities in the great outer court. The separation was emphasized when a line, a separating wall, isolated the lay brothers from the rest of the cloister.

The unvarying rigidity of the Cistercian cloister spread over Europe rather like Roman forts of an earlier period. The discoveries at Fountains (p33) demonstrating the prior design of the cloister before the main church are an indication of the importance attached to it by the builders (Gilyard Beer & Coppack, 1986). The Cistercian monastery saw the cloister at the peak of its development.

Friaries

The objectives of friars, of the mendicant (begging) orders, were so different that reform is hardly the right way to describe them. They were not committed to the contemplative life of monks but were rather evangelists who by their example of poverty and lack of property combined with vigorous preaching spread the word of God. Combating heresy was one of their original functions and their close relationship with the laity caused them to tread on the toes of the secular clergy with whom they were not popular. Their livelihood depended on begging, so evidently they had to be based in towns not in the chosen remoter sites of the reformed orders of monks. Far from avoiding the laity they

21 Rievaulx, Yorkshire. Air photograph of Cistercian abbey: refectory in foreground, cloister and nave of church beyond, crossing and eastern arm to right with infirmary cloister to south of this with original infirmary converted to abbot's house on right. Cambridge Collection

had to go out and seek them. There were four main orders of friars: Franciscan, Dominican, Carmelite and Augustinian (not to be confused with canons of the same name). Attention can be confined to the first two: grey friars and black friars, the names referring to the colour of their habits. Both were formed in the early thirteenth century.

Anyone who has tried to recover the plan of a friary by excavation will appreciate how its vagaries contrast with those of a normal monastery. The church consists of two parts: a spacious nave designed for preaching separated by a passage (the 'walking place') below a low lantern or tower and beyond this a narrow eastern arm containing quire and presbytery (**23**). It has no transepts to which to attach a cloister, which is separate from the church linked only with the cross passage. There is no provision for direct access to the quire from the dormitory for the first office.

The friar's cloister was quite different to that of the monks. The dormitory is usually in the range opposite the church while the refectory is in the east range. Sometimes the main buildings overflow into an adjoining smaller cloister. The adjoining two-storeyed ranges project over the alleys, turning them into ground-floor passages.

For the friars the cloister survives without a doubt but it has lost much of its significance; the symbiosis with the church has vanished. One could not have the Sunday procession coming in through one door to asperge the rooms in the cloister and then leave by the other to return to the quire binding as it were church and cloister into one unity. English friaries normally only have one door. The contrast is perhaps most vivid in the

22 Beaulieu abbey, Hampshire. Air photograph of Cistercian abbey with refectory converted to parish church, cloister and church beyond marked out and also its infirmary.
Cambridge Collection

great Portuguese monasteries of Alcobaça (Cistercian) and Batalha (Dominican) made famous by the visit of William Beckford while still in use at the end of the eighteenth century. It is not just the contrast in the architecture or the disposition of the buildings in the cloister but the row of confessionals made through the wall of the south alley (a north cloister) of the friars' church. This demonstrates the overriding importance of the souls of the laity to the friars in what was the most important private alley in a normal monastery. This is not to decry the great achievements of the friars in learning; Thomas Aquinas was a Dominican.

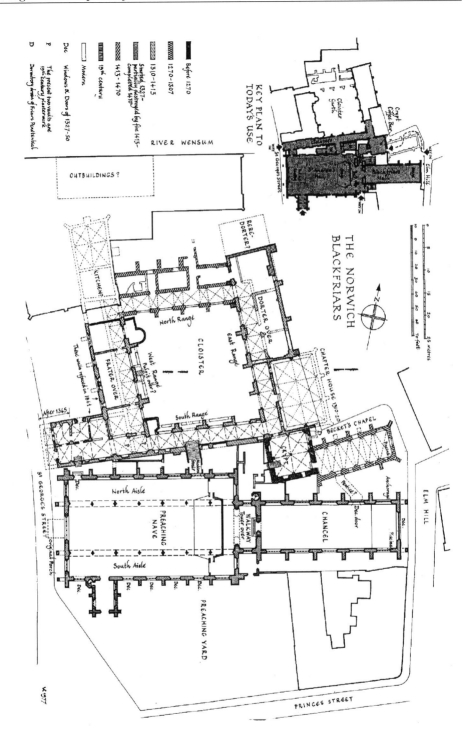

23 Norwich, plan of Blackfriars. Note division of church, dislocated position of cloister and quite different functions of ranges. Helen Sutermeister, Copyright Norwich City Council

The decline of the cloister

In the fifteenth and sixteenth centuries it was not so much the cloister that went out of use, for it seems to have been in working order (if sometimes dilapidated) right up to the Dissolution, but rather some of the buildings it served. Any generalisation has many exceptions but a few general points can be made.

In the East Midlands we have a fine set of published *Visitations 1437-43* (A.H. Thompson, 1919, 1927) by Bishop Alnwick for the diocese of Lincoln. Only Benedictine, Augustinian houses and Cistercian nunneries were subject to visitation so the reports are skewed. The most curious feature is that commonly the religious have divided up into three, four or five households (*domicilia*) centred on the infirmary, refectory, abbot's hall, misericord or guest house (e.g. 14, 114, 117 etc.). Clearly the monastic organisation was breaking up in these cases. Elsewhere we have our first information on the abandonment of the frater, most of the time in favour of the abbot's or prior's hall (Dorchester 72, Dunstable 83). This probably became general. At a large house, Peterborough, in 1437 there were 44 religious but only 10-12 in quire (iii p273). The abbot and four senior officers were excused all quire, two monks were at University, five only appeared on certain occasions, six lived at Oxeney, up to seven were being bled, and two or three were on the manors! The huge dormitory measuring 192 by 39ft must have been largely empty.

There are inventories for the sale of items from many West Midland houses (Walcott, 1871) and Peterborough in 1539 (Mellows, 1947). Apart from the church and chapter house household goods and furniture were in the hall, evidently the abbot's hall. At Thetford Cluniac priory the Register recently published (Dymond, 1995) indicated the same thing. The hall is presumably that in the west range of the cloister. The refectory was probably maintained and used for special feasts as was recalled in Elizabethan times at Durham (Fowler, 1903). There the religious all ate in the Loft at the west end of the refectory under the supervision of the second prior. Outside the refectory presumably the rules about silence, the reading of sacred texts, not eating meat and so on did not apply. The impression one receives is that there was a strong and growing resemblance between the situation in smaller monasteries and normal lay households with guests and religious all eating in the lord's, or here abbot's, hall.

By the time of the Dissolution the west range was in active use in Benedictine and Augustinian houses, the refectory remaining in a partly fossilised state and the dormitory divided up into separate cubicles but partly used. The chapter house was still in use. The position with Cistercians is less clear since the abbot's hall was outside the main cloister. At Rievaulx a detailed survey and inventory (*see* **46 & 47**) throws some light on this (Coppack, 1986). The abbot's hall was in the earlier infirmary but the surveyor saw the site in secular terms, treating this as if a normal hall. Clearly something similar to what was happening in houses of other orders had happened here. However one may doubt whether the cloister fared as well here as in other Cistercian abbeys, simply because the centre of use, the abbot's hall, was actually in the cloister in many smaller Benedictine or Augustinian houses.

Cloisters disappeared at the Dissolution with the rest of the monastery except of course where the church was a cathedral or became one: Norwich, Gloucester,

24 *Chester cathedral. The former abbey of St Werburgh, now the cathedral, the refectory and other parts of north cloister survive.* Cambridge Collection

Westminster and so on (**24**). These are fossilised but what would have happened to the cloister if there had been no Dissolution and the monasteries had gone on in use? We can make a guess from the bird's-eye views of French monasteries in the late seventeenth century in the *Monasticon Gallicanum* (Peigne-Delacourt, 1882). Cloisters are still recognisable but in a good many cases huge Renaissance or Baroque blocks exist, several stories high usually containing the dormitory as well as other elements. In its overpowering intention to impress, post-medieval architecture had less regard for function than appearance. The end of the cloister as the term is understood here was due as much to the change in style of architecture as to the accompanying changed attitudes towards monasticism and religious belief itself (**25, 50**).

3 The abbot in the monastery

The abbot in the monastery

The abbot is not simply the head of the dignitaries and officers of the abbey and president of the chapter of the monks . . . it is in him that above all resides the spiritual and temporal power of the monastic establishment. Passive obedience is owed him: he has total powers. He is called *dominus* and he alone from the beginning has the right to use a seal. Theoretically he can do nothing without consulting his chapter, in reality he enjoys absolute authority (Luchaire, 1892, 70).

The word 'abbot' is of Semitic, Syriac, origin although possibly its use for the head of house started with Coptic 'Apa' denoting respect or even reverence; its use reminds us of the oriental origin of monasticism. The other words for monastic officers are derived from Latin. Prior may be confusing: an abbot is usually the elected head of a large monastery and the prior the head of a smaller establishment, but the abbot had as his second in command a prior normally the executive head, who may be assisted by second, third or fourth priors. A further complication in England was that in monastic cathedrals (for example at Canterbury, Winchester, Ely Durham, Worcester and Rochester cathedrals) there was no abbot since the position of abbot was occupied by the bishops and the real executive and effective head of the monastery was the prior. The status of a prior of this kind was little different from that of an abbot so far as his way of life was concerned.

The Rule gave the abbot almost unlimited powers 'displaying the rigour of a master or the loving kindness of a father' (chapter 2), powers reinforced by the vow of obedience of the religious. Authority could be enforced by physical punishment (chapter 30) in chapter, various deprivations or humiliations, imprisonment in the abbot's prison or expulsion (chapter 28). We are not dealing therefore with a leader who had to rely on outside authority to enforce his will. One of the most fascinating subjects is to try to work out how far the abbot's position was recognised in terms of accommodation within the monastery. After all, in modern life a man's status is recognised by a hundred gradations of increasing comfort and luxury in every walk of present day life. In the monastic world there was a direct conflict between the degree of asceticism that monkhood implied and the worldly need to recognise status in the eyes of the religious, quite apart from the physical comfort of the abbot himself.

Our starting point can be the St Gall plan. As described above (p44) the abbot had his *aula abbatis*, abbot's hall or palace, two-storeyed with two rooms at each level. It is on the north side of the church with its own kitchen and latrines, a veritable mansion although probably shared with ecclesiastical guests (chapter 56: 'Let the abbot always eat with guests and pilgrims'). The situation can hardly be reconciled with decisions of synods of 816 and 817 at Aachen that the abbot should eat in the refectory and sleep in the company of at least six monks that is in the communal dormitory. Perhaps the donor of the plan wished Gozbert to adopt it by offering special accommodation for the abbot! Unfortunately we do not know whether what was shown on the plan represented current practice at the time the plan was made. Those who regard the plan as merely representing contemporary practice would imagine that is what the synods were inveighing against. Those who regard the plan as theoretical, or even utopian, that what was shown was imaginary and has no real bearing on where the abbot was accommodated at that time, would deny this.

At all events the synods may have had some influence, for the abbot is found back in the cloister in Cluny III not, it is true, in the dormitory in the east range but in the west range (Conant, 1968). The matter is of special interest for English students of monasticism since in England Benedictine and Augustinian heads of houses were firmly installed in the west range of the cloister by the twelfth century. An even more remarkable point is that Aethelwold in the tenth century revival under St Dunstan sent Osgar, a monk, to St Benoît-sur-Loire, Fleury, a Cluniac monastery near Orleans, to seek guidance on rebuilding the abbey of Abingdon (Stevenson, 1857). Fleury features in the *Monasticon Gallicanum*, which gives bird's-eye views of a large number of French monasteries in use at the end of seventeenth century (**25**). Most of the abbeys had long since been rebuilt and had a house for the abbot outside the cloister, but at Fleury the abbot was firmly installed in the west range with his garden to the south and a projection to the west. This was a rare case in the two volumes of illustrations. It does not mean that the abbot was already installed in the west range by the tenth century but it is fairly suggestive. If it were so it could mean the position of the abbot in English monasteries in the west range was established in pre-Norman times, brought back by Osgar from Fleury. Unfortunately there is no clear evidence that cloisters were already in use in England before the Norman Conquest; they were unsuited to multiple churches.

That abbots had a firm footing in the west range soon after the Conquest we know from the existence of the abbot's chapel over the outer parlour (at the entry to the cloister) at Westminster, Abingdon and Gloucester (Robinson, 1911, 35-6). At Westminster, the cloister was completed by Abbot Gilbert Crispin (1085-1117). Battle was founded by the Conqueror in thanks-giving for his success at the Battle of Hastings and appears to have had its abbot installed in the west range from the beginning (Brakspear, 1933).

A chamber in the west range does not mean the abbot slept there although with chamber and chapel it seems most likely that he did. On the other hand at Bec with which Archbishops Lanfranc and Anselm and Abbot Crispin had been closely associated before coming from Normandy the abbot slept in the dormitory at least in the mid-eleventh century (Robinson, 1911, 6). This might lend some credence to the suggestion that the use of the west range by the abbot was a pre-Conquest feature in England and was adopted by, rather than introduced by, the Normans. The rest of the first floor was presumably also a guest hall, the justification for the abbot's presence, and the ground floor no doubt remained a place for storage.

At all events wherever the Benedictine and Augustinian heads of houses acquired their habit of using the west range it is quite clear that the Cistercians could not do so as it was

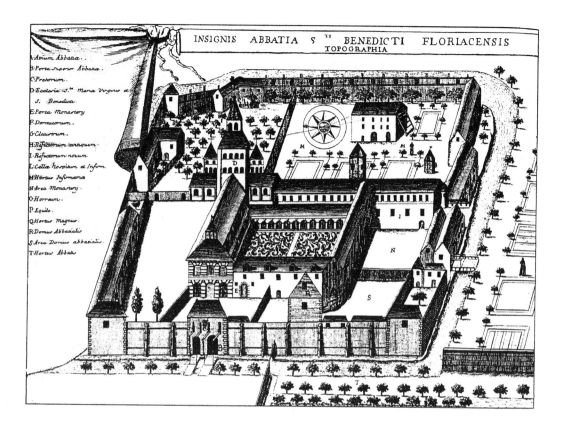

INSIGNIS ABBATIA S TI BENEDICTI FLORIACENSIS
TOPOGRAPHIA

A·Atrium Abbatiæ
B·Porta superior Abbatiæ
C·Prætorium
D·Ecclesia S.ta Maria Virginis et
      S. Benedicti
E·Porta Monasterij
F·Dormitorium
G·Claustrum
H·Refectorium antiquum
I·Refectorium novum
L·Cellæ hospitum et Infirm.
M·Hortus Infirmaria
N·Area Monasterij
O·Horreum
P·Equile
Q·Hortus Magnus
R·Domus Abbatialis
S·Area Domus abbatialis
T·Hortus Abbatis

*25 The abbey of Fleury, St Benoît-sur-Loire, a late seventeenth-century view: note abbot installed in
     west range with garden to south (R, S) as in English Benedictine fashion.* Peigne-Delacourt

now taken over by the lay-brothers, their workforce (p55). For a hundred years or more
Cistercian abbots (there were no Cistercian priories) lived in the east range in the
dormitory. There may have been some loss of dignity compared to the Benedictine abbots
but this perhaps corresponded better to what St Benedict had in mind and that after all
was the chief Cistercian objective.

There is no general agreement as to whereabouts within the range the Cistercian
abbots slept. Enlart in 1894 (p24), describing the great Italian Cistercian monasteries of
Fossanova and Casamari, wrote:

> The other extremity of the upper floor separated from the dormitory by the
> cloister stair contained the 'cellule' of the abbot and other dignitaries.

This is the southern end of the range but on the other hand another distinguished French
architectural historian in his work on the Cistercians in France puts the abbot at the north
end of the range in a little vaulted chamber projecting over the cloister walk (Aubert, 1947,
ii, 24). These little rooms are dark and seem more suitable for linen cupboards. Being

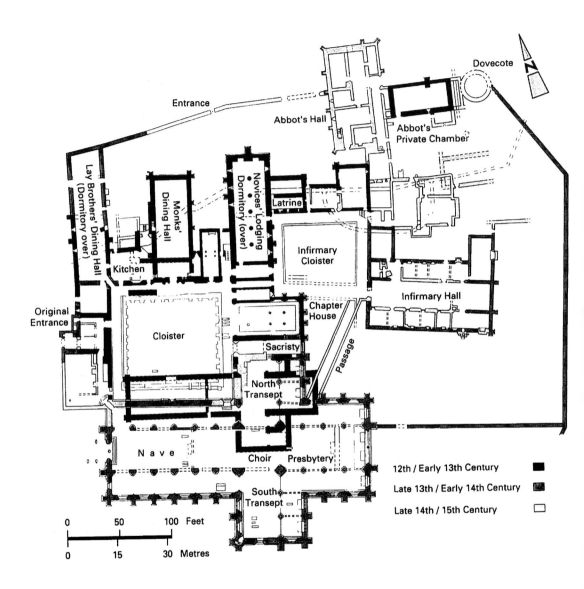

26 Tintern Abbey, Gwent. Cistercian house with north cloister. Note position of abbot's house, latrine culvert and infirmary on east. Cadw: Welsh Historic Monuments. Crown Copyright

beneath the bell on the transept that summoned the monks to first office this lay on a noisy thoroughfare.

Enlart's proposal fits the English evidence much better. The attraction of the convenience of the latrine on one side, the east, for the water channel ran this way and the warmth from the great fire in the adjoining warming room on the other side, the west, were surely overriding considerations, quite apart from the extra privacy afforded by that end (**26**). There is little doubt that in English Cistercian monasteries the abbot occupied the southern end of the east range.

During the day in winter the alley on the church side of the cloister, the north side in a southern cloister, had the sun but this cannot have been sufficient in cold weather to make it bearable. The warming house was the only heated room with its enormous fireplaces, except that is the kitchen. At Alcobaça Cistercian monastery in Portugal, one of the best preserved Cistercian churches and cloisters in Europe, the kitchen adjoins the dormitory (it is a north cloister, usual in Portugal) and still retains its huge central stove and great hood and central flue above. In the dormitory just north of the day stairs, which come up through the floor formed by the vault below, is a door which led to a room (now floorless) created over the kitchen with a central flue or chimney which must have heated it. This presumably was for the use of the abbot and illustrates the lengths to which steps might be taken to provide heat for those in the dormitory. Monks sleep in their habit but the cold in the dormitory must have been a severe trial. During offices or processions thick vestments could provide extra warmth.

The emergence of the abbot

The emergence of the abbot or prior either right out of the cloister or by the transformation of part of the cloister into a formal house for him occurred more or less all over Europe from the thirteenth century (Aubert, 1947, ii, 36, 90-1, 147-8). It was not quite a return to St Gall since the new accommodation was not on the other side of the church (**27**).

Appendix I is an attempt to divide cloisters into two categories based on those where the published plans yield sufficient information: a) cloisters where the abbot's house was either in the west range or west or south of that range; b) those where the abbot's house was east or south-east of the eastern or dormitory range. While the lists are not exhaustive there are a number of points that stand out for discussion.

First it is clear that for Benedictines, Augustinian and Premonstratensian canons the abbot's or priors house was either a development in the west range or a new construction to the west of it, while for the Cistercians it was almost invariably a new construction on the east side (**28**). There are many exceptions to be discussed below but the regulars are sufficiently numerous to allow us to draw the general conclusion that heads of houses were in these different ranges before the thirteenth century, and perhaps indeed from the foundation of the house. I have to some extent jumped the gun in the earlier part of this chapter by assuming this.

Let us now turn to the exceptions, which have considerable interest. There was of course no obligation on the part of an abbot to follow normal practice. For example at

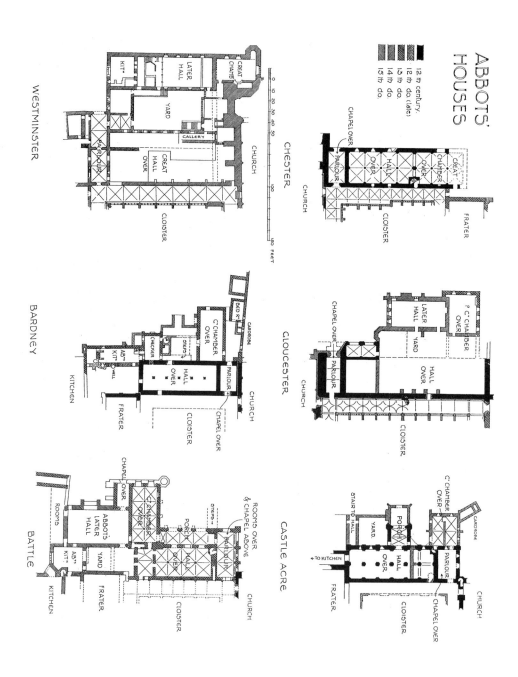

27 *Comparison of abbots' houses in west range of cloister at Benedictine monasteries.*
H. Brakspear, *Archaeologia* 83

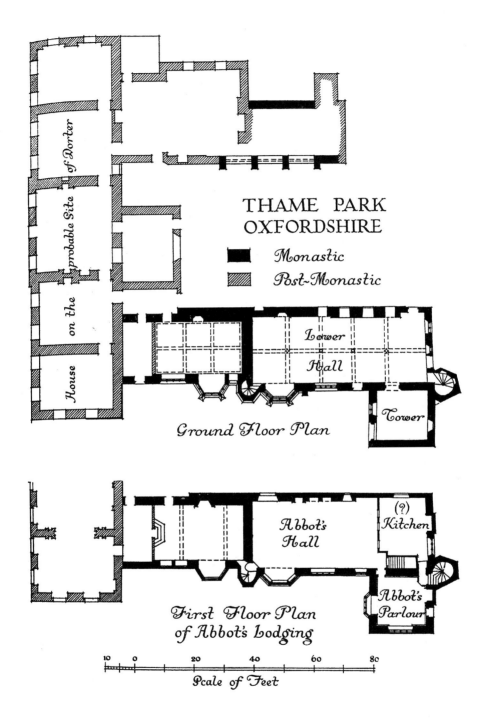

THAME PARK
OXFORDSHIRE

■ *Monastic*

▨ *Post-Monastic*

probable Site of Dorter

House on the

Lower Hall

Tower

Ground Floor Plan

Abbot's Hall

(?) Kitchen

Abbot's Parlour

First Floor Plan of Abbot's Lodging

10 0   20   40   60   80

Scale of Feet

28 *Thame Park, Oxon. Surviving abbot's house from Cistercian abbey projecting from east range.*
Godfrey, *Archaeological Journal 86*

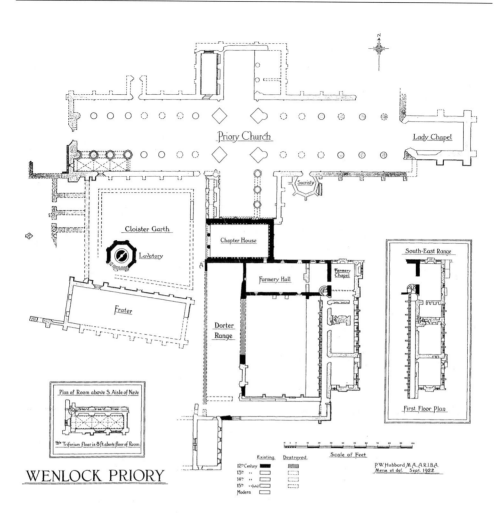

29 Much Wenlock, Shropshire. Cluniac priory showing position of prior's house in infirmary cloister. D.S. Cranage, *Archaeologia 72*

Much Wenlock Cluniac priory (Cluniac is essentially a form of Benedictinism but with central control from Cluny) it may be suspected that the prior was established in the west range but that possibly following his elevation by 'mitring' by the pope (discussed below p100) he decided to build that handsome and famous house to the east of the east range in the infirmary cloister that is still occupied to this day (**29-32**). The Benedictine exceptions in list B are interesting since they are mainly in the north of England where we may suspect there was strong influence from the great Cistercian abbeys. If the site of the abbot's house at the Benedictine abbey of St Mary's York really lies under the King's Manor, now York University, this could be a remarkable case of Cistercian influence and ironical in view of the origins of Cistercian Fountains from there. Tynemouth Benedictine priory is most remarkable since the west range first floor became the 'common hall' while

30 Wenlock priory, prior's house, elevation into infirmary cloister. J. Parker

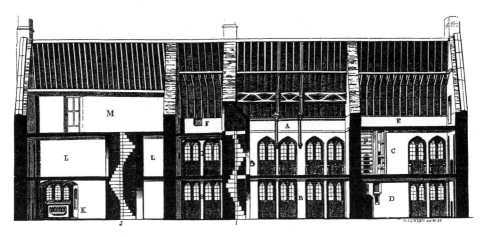

SECTION OF THE ABBOT'S HOUSE, WENLOCK ABBEY.

A *The Hall, or Refectory, with its roof.*	G *Apartment, with locker.*	L *Apartment modernised.*
B *Kitchen.*	H *Ditto.*	M *Ditto.*
C *The Abbot's Parlour*	I *Staircase leading to all three stories.*	N *Garderobe.*
D *Brewhouse.*	J *Ditto, leading to the gallery and prin-*	O *Ditto.*
E *Dormitory.*	*cipal rooms.*	P *Staircase leading to the Abbot's Dormitory.*
F *Dormitory in the roof.*	K *Oratory, with altar.*	

31 Wenlock priory, prior's house in section. Note hall at A. J. Parker

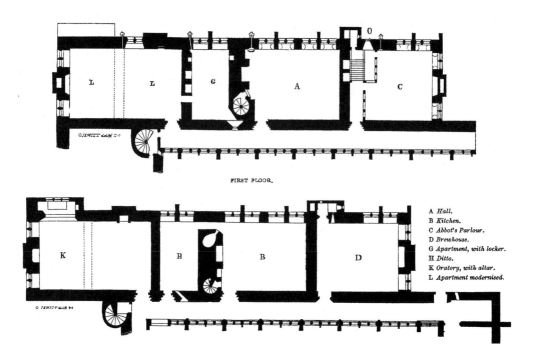

32 Wenlock priory, ground plan of prior's house. J. Parker

the prior moved to the southern end of the east range the original position of a Cistercian abbot. Tynemouth is of course peculiar in that it shared the promontory with a castle. Bury St Edmunds, Suffolk, was different in that it had frequent royal visits and the east range was extended northwards (a north cloister) to form a veritable country-house façade facing the main entry with the back overlooking the stream (**33 & 34**).

To some extent the exceptions among the Augustinians may have the same explanation. At Bolton abbey, Yorkshire the old abbot's house was in the west range and was then moved (**35**). There was perhaps a tendency for cloisters on the north side to be irregular like Lesnes, Kent where the reasons for putting the cloister on the north (gradients and drainage) might equally suggest a different site for the abbot's or prior's lodging.

What is of great interest is the rarity of exceptions among Cistercian houses like the cases of Robertsbridge in Sussex or Forde in Dorset. The west range had been occupied from foundation in the twelfth century but when the lay brothers disappeared in the fourteenth century it was too late to take over the range; in any case by that time the abbot had probably left the cloister all together. The drainage — the latrine culvert east or south east of the range — simplified those arrangements and sometimes the abbot's house was actually built over the culvert as at Fountains. At Thame Park, Oxfordshire, the east range is now occupied by later buildings but the abbot's hall and chamber extend eastwards almost as if seeking the culvert (**28**) (Godfrey, 1930)! The infirmary was east of the range and in some cases, like Furness and Rievaulx, a superseded infirmary was taken over as the abbot's house.

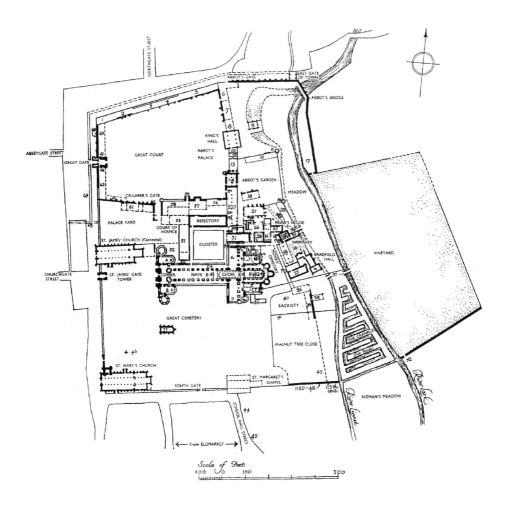

33 Bury St Edmunds, plan of the Benedictine monastery. A.B. Whittingham, *Archaeological Journal* 106

Before turning to the buildings themselves it may be helpful to discuss the reasons for the abbot or prior wishing to 'emerge' from the cloister. One of the changes at the Norman Conquest was the imposition of military tenure on the greater monasteries so the abbot held the abbey supplying the king with a fixed number of knights (Chew, 1932). This was not simply a paper transaction for we know from Jocelyn that the knights were a rather disruptive element at Bury St Edmunds. If the abbot was to the treated like a feudal lord then surely he ought to live like one. The fact that he had to eat with guests and entertain them constantly rubbed this in. There were two kinds of life in the monastery, that enjoyed by guests and knights and the ascetic life of the monks themselves. No wonder the abbot felt that the former, which he to some extent already enjoyed, required his own establishment if only as a mark of his status.

34 Bury St Edmunds, views of abbot's house in 1720 and 1803. K. Yates, 1843

In England there was a potent additional factor: a substantial number of cathedrals were also Benedictine monasteries (Augustinian in the case of Carlisle). In these cases this was the bishop's see, seat, and he lived in a palace outside the cloister although he held the abbot's position in some respects (M.W. Thompson, 1998). He often was not a monk. Among the early works carried out by Archbishop Lanfranc, who was a monk from Bec and abbot at Caen, was to construct himself a house at Canterbury near the west range of the cloister at Christchurch where he presumably would have lived had he been the abbot. All the bishops' palaces were outside the cloister.

A most interesting case is Henry of Blois, bishop of Winchester, 1129-71, who had been brought over from Cluny by Henry I to be abbot of Glastonbury and who was subsequently elected to the see of Winchester but retained the abbacy, holding both posts concurrently. Although he was an absentee abbot for much of the time he built among other structures at Glastonbury a house for himself that was nicknamed 'the castle', perhaps a two-storey square keep-like structure that I have called a 'protokeep' in the case of the example at Winchester, possibly built also by Henry of Blois. It was probably not a military building but two sets of hall and chamber at two levels — 'flats' or 'maisonettes' for guests. Excavations at Thetford priory have revealed something similar (**36**), part of which was later incorporated into prior's lodging attached to the west range (Wilcox, 1982). Bishop Henry's work at Glastonbury, the premier abbey, must have been widely known and one that was no doubt envied.

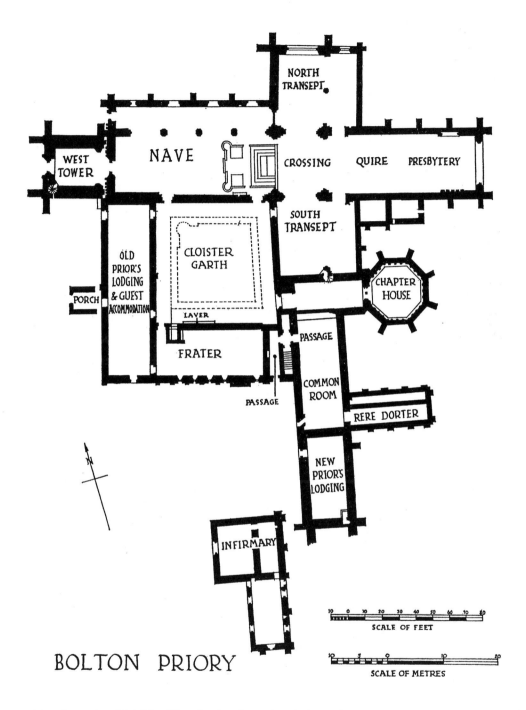

35 Bolton priory, Yorkshire. Plan showing change in prior's quarters.
   A.H. Thompson, *Publications of Thoresby Society* 30

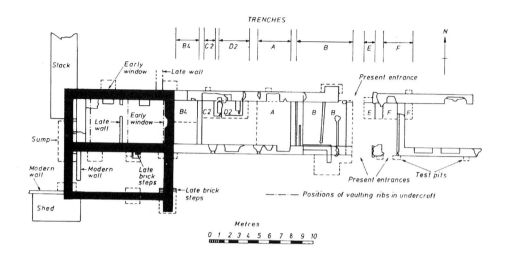

36 *Thetford priory, the square building ('proto-keep') discovered in excavation partly incorporated into westward extension to west range for prior's lodging.* R. Wilcox, *Norfolk Archaeology* 40

Ely is a particularly interesting case since it was given cathedral status only in 1109. We may suspect that the abbot had been living in the west range in the normal way but protocol now required him to leave the cloister. He did not go very far since the bishop's palace is only a short distance to the west. In monastic cathedrals the prior, now executive head, had something of the status of an abbot and lived like one (priors of Durham, Ely, Canterbury etc.), but he was not privileged to move into the abbot's quarters in the west range. He had to remain south of the cloister in the normal position of the prior as at Westminster. The classic case is Ely with its splendid range of halls to be mentioned below (p89).

Abbots' and priors' houses in the monastery

Strictly speaking there is no such thing as a type of dwelling that is specially that of an abbot. The abbot or prior had no concept of a form of house exclusively designed for himself, but copied the contemporary layman's house in so far as resources and the circumstances of the site allowed. There is no real classification that can be made. It is hoped that the figures will give a general idea of the sort of domestic arrangement they made within the monastery.

Brakspear's article on Battle (1933) showed six examples of the development of abbots' or priors' houses in the west range of the cloister in five Benedictine and one Cluniac house (*see* **27**). At Chester, a northern cloister, the original twelfth-century arrangement has hardly altered (*see* **24**). The outer parlour adjoins the church at the south end with the abbot's chapel over. Then follows the first-floor rooms, presumably conceived of as a guest hall, as the abbot's own hall and his chamber. The western cloister alley adjoins immediately on the right.

At Gloucester the cloister was again a northern one and later expansion took place by building on the west side. A new ground-floor hall and a two-storey chamber suite were built to the west in the fourteenth century, separated by a small yard from the west range. The west alley of the cloister with its famous fifteenth-century vault adjoins on the east side.

At Castle Acre priory, Norfolk, a Cluniac house, the cloister is on the south and the west range is largely intact with outer parlour beneath prior's chapel at the north end (**37-40**). There were extensive additions to the first floor to the west on an original twelfth-century porch and at the north end handsome chambers, one with a well-known bow window (**38**).

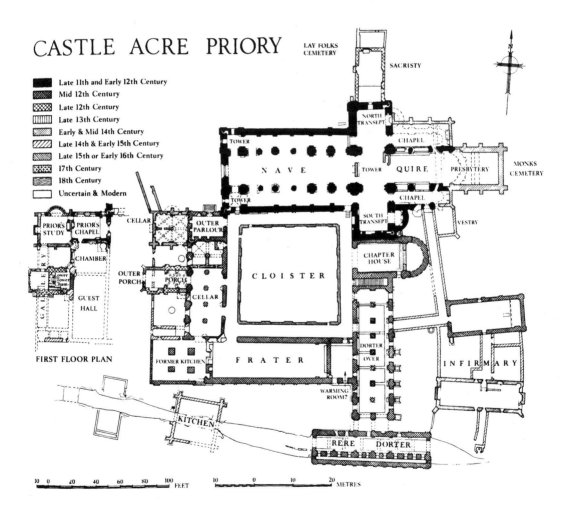

37 Castle Acre priory, Norfolk, plan of Cluniac monastery. Note prior's apartments in west range.
NMR. Crown Copyright

38 Castle acre priory: west end of Church and prior's lodging adjoining it with its oriel window. A.E. Thompson

39 Castle Acre priory: entry to prior's apartments in west range. A.E. Thompson

40 Castle Acre priory: view across cloister to west tower of church and prior's lodging in west range.
A.E. Thompson

At Thetford, another Norfolk Cluniac priory (not illustrated by Brakspear), excavation revealed a 'proto-keep', probably a guesthouse; the larger northern part formed the west end of an extension from the west range, no doubt adding a chamber to the existing accommodation (Wilcox, 1982) (**36**).

At Westminster the whole arrangement was redesigned by Abbot Littlington in the fourteenth century when the west end of the abbey church was completed, so there is little of the original work visible (Widmore, 1751, 102). The western alley of the cloister was realigned, the old first-floor hall removed and a new range created with a chamber at the west end of the abbey serving a ground-floor hall with kitchen to the south. To the east were a yard, a gallery and then the site of the original hall (**41**). The outer parlour at its southern end at the entry to the cloister was rebuilt.

At Bardney Abbey, Lincolnshire, excavation of the west range has demonstrated a first-floor hall and chapel at its north were supplemented by a great chamber at the north end which projected westwards in the thirteenth century (**42**).

At Battle Abbey, Sussex, the first-floor hall of the thirteenth century constructed with its great chamber projecting west was supplemented or replaced by a ground-floor hall to the south in the fifteenth century (*see* **8**). What these plans show is adaptation of the original design to accord with the changing demands made of domestic arrangement in the lay world outside the cloister without actually disturbing the normal functioning of the cloister.

41 Westminster abbey, plan. Note complete reconstruction of abbot's lodging to the west of west range in the fourteenth century.
Royal Commission on Historic
Monuments, NMR, Crown Copyright

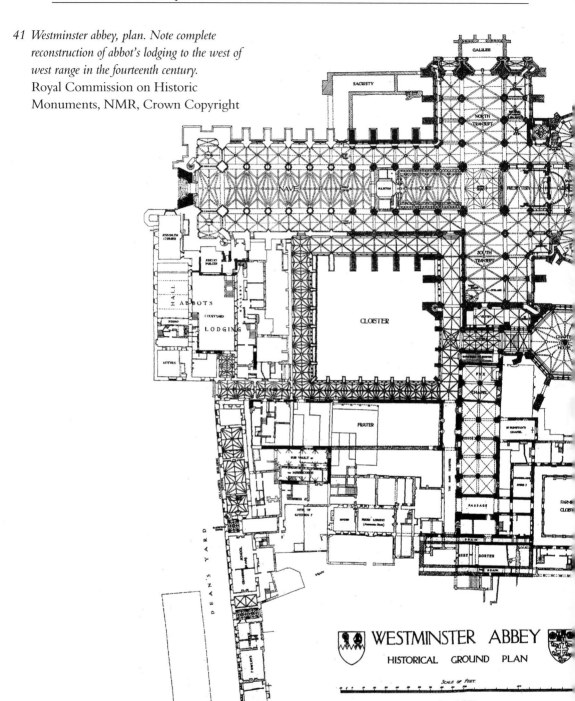

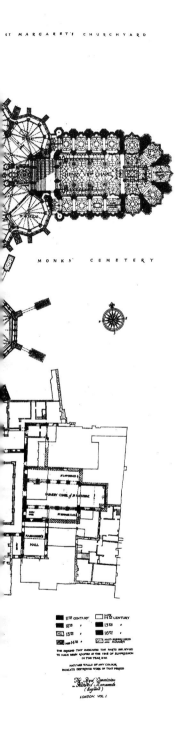

MONKS' CEMETERY

At Bradenstoke Priory, an Augustinian house, a print of the west range in use after the Dissolution but before its destruction shows how this range of the cloister readily lent itself to domestic use (**43**). The east side of Bury St Edmunds north transept was extended to the north for the abbot with chamber and first-floor hall (p74) and beyond a later aisled hall, the King's Hall (*see* **33 & 34**). The sequence of construction recalls that just described at other Benedictine houses.

Plans of abbot's lodgings completely free of the cloister, other than Cistercian, are less common. At the Augustinian abbey of Haughmond, Shropshire, the hall and chamber on the south side of the cloister at first regarded as an infirmary are now interpreted as a normal hall and chamber accommodation for the abbot (Emery, 2000, ii, fig. 130).

The most dramatic and most frequently quoted prior's house is at the Cluniac priory at Much Wenlock, Shopshire, now privately inhabited (**29-32**). The prior who had been promoted (mitred) by the pope in the fifteenth century decided to leave the west range and set himself up in a new building east of the east range adjoining the infirmary. The striking feature of this building is the fenestration facing into the infirmary cloister along corridors at both floor levels, two pairs of round-headed lights set between each buttress. At each level there were three divisions, services and chambers on the ground floor with the main hall on the first floor (Emery, 2000, ii, fig. 141), again flanked at either end by chambers. It is a small but impressive hall with a fine decorated roof of three bays. The absence of the normal winged development of lay domestic architecture and corridors seem to ally it more with medieval inns or lodgings ranges. There is no question that it is an outstanding piece of architecture.

One might cite further examples of Benedictine and Augustinian abbots' lodgings, but sufficient has been said to demonstrate the principles. There were grander examples like Peterborough, now the bishop's palace but much altered in the nineteenth century. It stood south-west of the west range but he still used the hall in the range. In a position recalling this at Muchelney, Somerset, west of the refectory, is a very

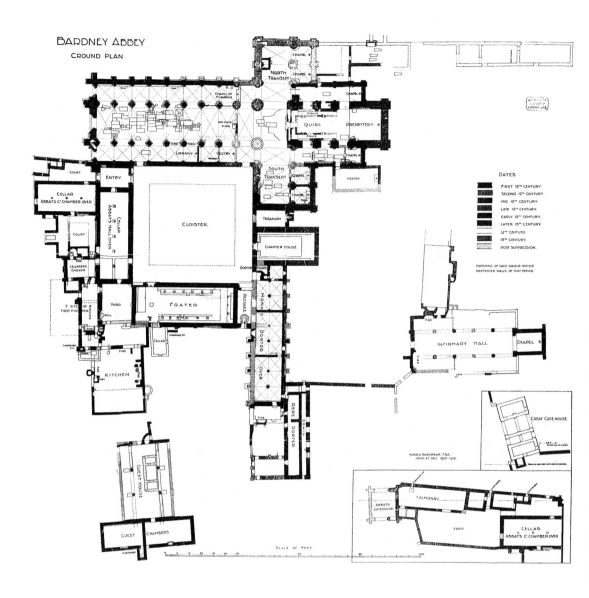

42 Bardney Abbey, Lincolnshire, plan of Benedictine monastery. Note additions to west range for abbot's lodging and also plan of fourteenth-century great gate. H. Brakspear, *Archaeological Journal* 79

43 Bradenstoke Augustinian priory, Wiltshire. The west range still inhabited after the Dissolution but before demolition

fine set of rooms with a decorated late medieval ceiling, fireplace and wall paintings, built by the Benedictine abbot. These are in the care of English Heritage and can be visited.

Turning attention to abbots who emerged from the east range, the Cistercian abbey of Croxden, Staffordshire, is a good example albeit only surviving as foundations (**44**). The east range was extended to the south by two bays over the latrine culvert in the thirteenth century to accommodate the abbot, and in the fourteenth century he apparently moved to the south-east. It is an almost classical sequence. At Jervaulx (**45**) the southern end of the range had a rectangular building erected on it with a chapel although the abbot later moved out to the east. Identification of function is not always easy from mere foundations.

Another course for the Cistercian abbot to take was to take over the infirmary, two examples of which are Furness, Lancashire and Rievaulx, Yorkshire. At Furness the thirteenth-century infirmary, a two-storey structure, was adapted for this purpose and a new infirmary built. A late fifteenth-century 'proto-keep', probably guesthouse, adjoins the dormitory range (p77), possibly on the site of an early move by the abbot. At Rievaulx the abbot installed himself in the original one-aisled, twelfth-century infirmary hall, which was divided up into two parts. Detailed survey, inventory and ministers' accounts survive from the Dissolution describing not only the buildings but what was in them (usually empty) (Coppack, 1986) (**46 & 47**). The surveyor treats it as if it were a normal secular hall.

At Fountains the abbot's house, over a prison and the latrine culvert, seems too small for the abbot of such a large and famous abbey. At Tintern, Gwent, the cloister is on the

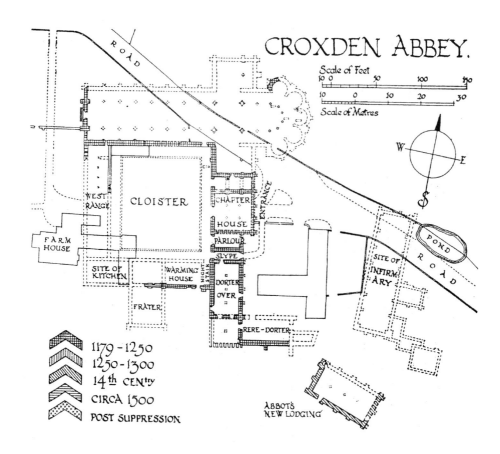

CROXDEN ABBEY.

Scale of Feet

Scale of Metres

W — E

S

ROAD

CLOISTER

WEST RANGE

CHAPTER

HOUSE

PARLOUR

SLYPE

ENTRANCE

FARM HOUSE

SITE OF KITCHEN

WARMING HOUSE

NIGHT STAIR

DORTER OVER

FRATER

RERE-DORTER

POND

ROAD

SITE OF INFIRMARY

1179 – 1250
1250 – 1300
14th CENty
CIRCA 1500
POST SUPPRESSION

ABBOTS NEW LODGING

44 Croxden abbey, Staffordshire: east range extended in the thirteenth and fourteenth centuries to create separate quarters for the abbot in Cistercian fashion. NMR, Crown Copyright

north side and a quite distinct and elaborate first-floor hall and chamber were constructed (*see* **26**).

The abbot's special responsibilities for guests mean that is not always clear whether a building ostensibly a guesthouse was not in fact partly occupied by the abbot himself. At Kirkstall abbey near Leeds in Yorkshire the buildings underwent a remarkable development, ending up like a large secular house one might have thought too grand for guests only (**48**; Coppack , 1990, 104). It is often cited as the Cistercian example of a guesthouse changed into something like that of a rich merchant of the period.

It will have been noticed that most of the abbots' houses in monasteries that have been described are very late, sometimes only a few years before the Dissolution of the monasteries in 1536-9. Three examples that dramatically illustrate this are from the county of Dorset and can be studied in the *Royal Commission on Historic Monuments* inventory volumes for Dorset (I, p73 and p240, iii, pt. 2, p191). Forde Abbey in the extreme west of the county was a Cistercian foundation with a new house built by Abbot

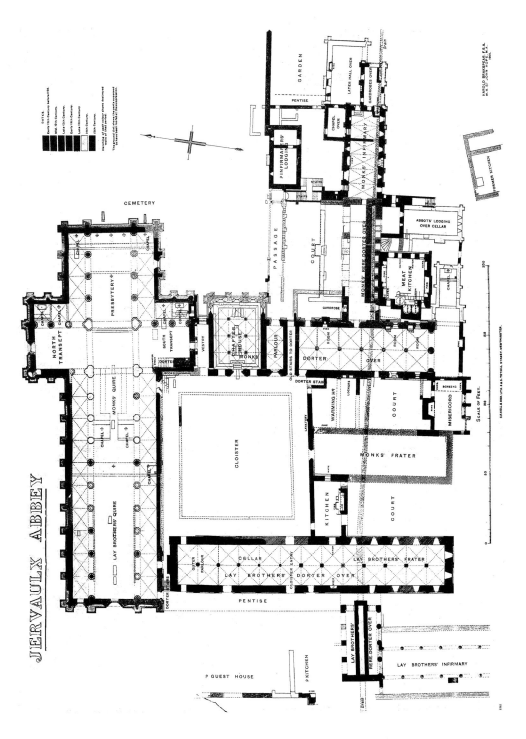

45 Jervaulx abbey, Yorkshire: Cistercian house with additions to the east range replaced by a later building for the abbot. Brakspear and Hope, *Yorkshire Archaeological Journal 21*

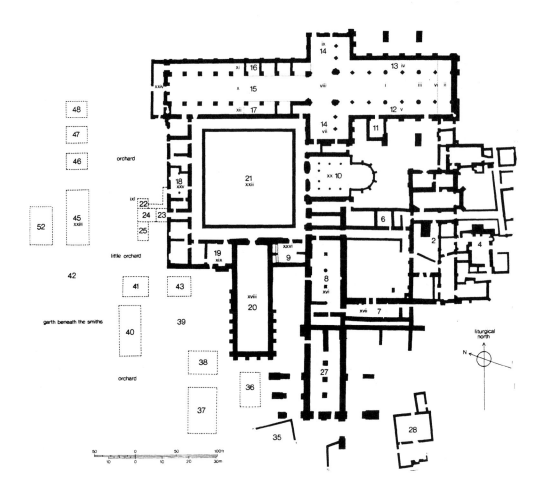

46 Rievaulx abbey, plan of Cistercian monastery at Dissolution with former infirmary converted into abbot's hall at 2. G. Coppack, Journal of the British Archaeological Association 139

Chard in 1528, the date recorded on its splendid three-storey porch. The great hall itself has four-light windows and inside its original king-post roof later concealed by a ceiling below. The church, which has disappeared, had a northern cloister and the abbot's hall was most irregularly set at the north-west corner of the west range. Milton Abbey was a Benedictine house and equally irregular with Abbot Middleton's hall (*c.*1498) set east of the east range (now incorporated into a later mansion). It has a splendid arch-braced roof and screen but altered exterior. At Cerne Abbey only the magnificent three-storey porch with bow-windows (oriels) at the two upper levels, resembling that at Forde, has survived, the work of abbot Thomas Sam (1497-1509). Both Forde and Milton have survived because they continued in use after the Dissolution. Why were abbots building so grandly just before it; not I think as a kind of *après moi la deluge*, a last gamble. More probably it is related to the secular style of life, much closer to that of a lay lord, then being adopted in

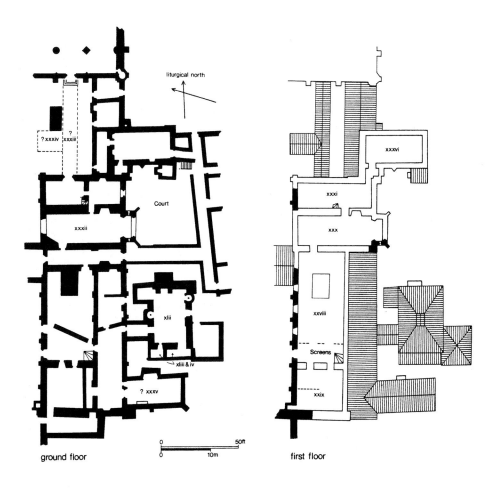

liturgical north

? xxxiv | xxxiii

Court

xxxii

xlii

xliii & iv

? xxxv

ground floor

xxxvi

xxxi

xxx

xxviii

Screens

xxix

first floor

0   50ft
0   10m

*47 Rievaulx abbey, showing how infirmary was transformed into abbot's lodgings in later middle
ages. G. Coppack, Journal of the British Archaeological Association 139*

monasteries (p59). Although the architecture is entirely traditional the Renaissance was
making itself felt in more than a hint of self-consciousness and self-identity that played so
great a part in behaviour long before it seriously affected architectural style or even detail.

This chapter cannot be concluded without reference to the prior's buildings at Ely.
After 1109 the abbot was replaced by a bishop at Ely and so the prior took on a new dignity
as at Durham, Winchester and Canterbury (Christchurch) cathedrals — a new status of
quasi-abbot. The remarkable set of buildings built for him must be the most complete set
of domestic buildings in an abbey that survive (**49**) (Atkinson, 1933; Holton-Krayenbuhl,
2000). It is a complicated sequence starting with a first-floor hall for the Prior from the
early twelfth century, a range of two-storey lodgings against the perimeter wall and the
monks' kitchen to the south of their refectory (the whole complex is south of this). One
might have expected the prior to be in the dormitory in the early twelfth century so

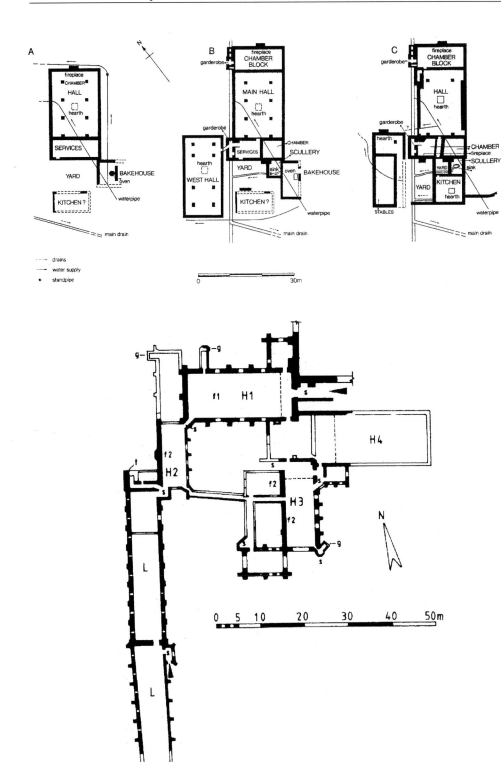

48 (left, top) Kirkstall abbey, near Leeds, showing the conversion in this Cistercian house of the guesthouse into a winged secular-type hall house. G. Coppack, Abbeys and Priories, 1990, fig. 67

49 (left, bottom) Ely cathedral (priory), the final form at first-floor level of the prior's lodging/ guesthouse as discussed in text (p89). A. Holtion-Krayenbuhl, Archaeological Journal 156

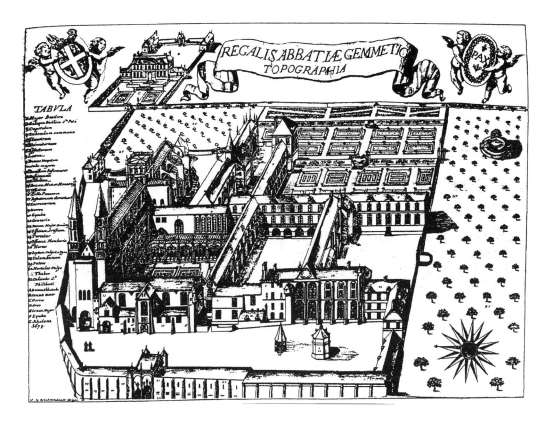

50 (above) Jumièges, Seine-inferieure, a late seventeenth-century view of the monastery. Note the abbot's baroque mansion at top left near the scroll. Peigne-Delacourt

possibly this started as a guesthouse, like for instance those at Fountains. The sequence ended up with three first-floor halls all interlinked at first floor-level and a ground-floor hall perhaps replacing or supplementing the prior's original hall. In addition the prior had a small but charming little chapel attributed to Prior Crauden. The functions attributed to the hall are guesthouses, H1 and H2, and the prior's quarters, H3 and H4. The abbot's duties with regard to guests presumably devolved to the prior when the abbot had been elevated to bishop.

This happy survival illustrates the difficulty of disentangling abbot's or prior's quarters from those of guests. The Ely group constitutes by far the most important surviving set of monastic secular domestic buildings. Unfortunately it does not lend itself to photography and most of it is indeed inaccessible, being occupied by the bishop and King's School, Ely.

4 The abbot outside the monastery

The abbot outside the monastery

Abbots had many reasons for leaving the abbey since the time of Pachomius and in this country from Saxon times. The abbot who had to go to Rome for confirmation of his election started off his period of office with several months' absence. The Orders created in the twelfth century normally expected their heads of houses to attend annual 'chapters' of houses at the mother house. Cistercian abbots had this duty; we know from the pages of Matthew Paris that general chapters actually took place, for example in 1251 (Giles, 1852, ii 460). There were other reasons for leaving the monastery: business reasons in connection with its property, legal disputes, courts or like Abbot Samson looking into repairs of buildings. The late Dom Knowles (1966, I, 301) remarked how abbots grew away from the religious in their houses in the early twelfth century, becoming more and more preoccupied with business or even national affairs.

Jocelyn of Brokeland's famous biography of Abbot Samson of Bury St Edmunds (1182-1211) must be one of the main sources for heads of house at the end of the twelfth and beginning of the thirteenth centuries with its wealth of information on his activities both before and after his exciting election to the post in 1182 (Butler, 1949). Abbot Robert II (elected 1102) probably completed the cloister with the 'abbot's hall', possibly here meaning in the west range. He also made a division between the property belonging to the abbot and that belonging to the monks, an important distinction since during a vacancy the abbot's property was held by the Crown until a new election, while the property of the monks remained with them. This gave the abbot considerable independence and freedom of movement. Samon was already active before his election being concerned with construction of the great west tower of the abbey church. Shortly after his election Samson began restoring 'old halls and ruinous houses through which kites and crows were flying', and he took a very active part in organising the manors. In places where there had been only barns he added houses. He preferred to live on the manors to avoid the worries of the abbey; according to Jocelyn he spent more time away from the abbey than he did in it. He was 'mitred' by the pope giving him quasi-episcopal status. He became involved in international affairs: he visited Richard I then held captive in Germany with demands for a ransom; Samson undertook negotiations. He carried arms during the siege of Windsor, an irregular and improper activity for a monk. In a way he serves as a pattern of a forceful but not very spiritual abbot of the future: long absent from the monastery, travelling around his manor houses, occasionally involved in public affairs, and also, of course, periods at the abbey of which he was head. There one of his main duties was to entertain guests, which in the case of Bury St Edmunds not uncommonly meant the king.

No comprehensive list of manor houses of a monastery used by heads of houses on their travels can be drawn up: there were far too many monasteries as the published list of Knowles and Hadcock (1972) shows and the abbots of the larger monasteries certainly had dozens if not scores of such manor houses. In any case it is probable that only a few have surviving data to allow this to be attempted, as is clearly the case with Westminster Abbey. The churches and properties mentioned by Jocelyn (Butler, 1949, 63) give a clue as to the sort of numbers of houses available to Abbot Samson. We are evidently talking in thousands for all monastic houses. In Appendix II no attempt has been made to give full lists except to some degree at Westminster. Houses where an event shows the abbot using it or a few from Platt's list of granges (1969) where a head of house might have stayed have been included as well as one or two houses where there is a description or survey. The houses clearly did not differ significantly from laymens' houses and usually were not on a very grand scale, compared with those of bishops for example.

The itineraries that are the places visited, usually established by the locations given on documents, are much easier to establish for bishops from their registers than for abbots. At Westminster where the abbey's records largely survived the Dissolution an incomplete itinerary has been worked out for Abbot Walter de Wenlok (1283-1307) by Barbara Harvey (1965). He was abroad for two periods, as far as Rome for confirmation of his election in 1284, and in France for six months in 1291. A fairly complete itinerary was possible for the high winter months of January and February 1291. Places where he definitely had a house are shown with an asterisk.

January	1-2	Morton Foliot (Castelmorton, Worcs.)
	8	*Pershore (Worcs.)
	9	*Sutton under Brailes (Warwicks.)
	10	*Islip (Oxon.)
	11	Birchets Green (Berks.)
	12-13	*Laleham (Middx.)
	14	*Aldenham (Herts.)
	15-16	Berkhamstead (Herts.)
	16	*Aldenham
	17-19	*Westminster
	20-23	Battersea
	24-29	*Westminster
	30-31	*Laleham
February	1-2	Birchets Green
	3	Middleton Stoney (Oxon.)
	4-5	*Islip
	7	Enstone (Oxon.)
	8-10	*Todenham (Glos.)
	11-12	*Islip
	13	Hurley (Berks.)
	14-18	*Laleham
	19-22	*Westminster
	23-24	Charlton (Middx.)

These travels took place at the height of winter which seems to have been no deterrent to normal movement at this date (**51**).

This incessant travelling, a peripatetic existence, recalls that of bishops discussed elsewhere (Thompson, 1998). The houses were certainly not so grand as those of bishops — abbot's houses were hardly ever called 'palaces' as was quite common with those of bishops. The links with the monastery of which he was head were closer than those of a bishop with his cathedral; even in this short itinerary it can be seen that the abbot kept on returning to Westminster Abbey. At a slightly later date he would have stayed in Chelsea at La Neyte (Rutton, 1910), but the complete reconstruction of the abbot's house in the abbey later in the fourteenth century (Robinson, 1911) reminds us of the enduring bond between abbot and abbey.

How far was this peripatetic life general for heads of houses? In all the larger Benedictine houses it was probably normal, but smaller houses no doubt lacked the resources for travelling on this scale. As for the other Orders it is difficult to say: there are hints from an annual account of the Cistercian abbey of Beaulieu, Hampshire, that the abbot was a traveller (Hockey, 1975), but the evidence is probably not available for a clear picture.

There is no doubt that by Tudor times the senior heads of houses were living most of the time on manors only occasionally going to the monastery for special feast days. This is well illustrated by Prior William More of Worcester (this was a bishop's see so the prior acted as abbot) who has left a remarkable *Journal* for 1518-35 (Fegan, 1914), essentially a weekly statement of his expenses and receipts divided up into quarters of the year of 13 weeks each. Most of the time he spent at his manor houses of Grimley, Crowle and Battenhall near Worcester, only going to the monastery on special feast days like Christmas and Easter. He went to London once a year mainly for shopping. The abundant information on how he spent his time is remarkable. The cleaning of moats at Crowle (trapeze-shaped, 111 x 91 x 82 x 94 yards and 10 yards deep), presumably enclosing the house, is fascinating. The wealth of information cannot be described here. The impression one has, compared to Walter of Wenlock 200 years earlier, is that he was not constantly on the move but regarded the houses at the three manors as permanent homes for long residence on each visit, not just temporary halts.

The abbot's household (*hospicium*)

Abbot Walter of Wenlock's travels have just been described; we are fortunate that a set of instructions for members of his household drawn up in 1295 has survived in the Westminster abbey library. A transcription of the French text was published in 1920 by Pearce (1920, 106-12) and again in 1965 by Harvey (1965, 241-7); I have ventured to make a translation in Appendix III. It is especially relevant to our discussion.

It is not necessary to go through the whole document although the reader may well find it interesting to do so. At first sight it may be cause for surprise that an abbot should require such a large number of laymen permanently in his service ('liveried'). It will be appreciated that the sort of peripatetic life lived by Abbot Walter that has just been described required a considerable body of people to underpin it. There were no public services, no hotels or railways: all had to be arranged for the abbot by his own staff.

51 Westminster abbey, eighteenth-century view of great gatehouse from inside, the left-hand archway leading to the abbot's house. Demolished 1776

First is money: how it was raised and passed through various hands to maintain the household in its proper dignity. Account-keeping was essential when there were many sticky fingers about. The nightly audit with its physical punishment or expulsion for grave lapses reminds one of rather similar procedures in the daily chapter in the abbey. A 'livery' is the entitlement to board and lodging with certain perquisites, a horse and a gown, more fully listed at the end. The prevention of fraud and irregular claims to livery was one of the main concerns since this was the main form of expenditure; the quantities of foodstuffs and drink purchased being directly related to the number of liveries to be met.

The number of horses and the extraordinary care they required is a reminder of the mobility of the household. The rules were not intended for a particular place but for whichever of the houses (curt = court, the whole group of buildings) the abbot and household found themselves in. Clearly there was a fair degree of uniformity in the houses, all hall, chamber and service buildings. It is indeed one of the most instructive documents to illustrate the 'hall culture' at its peak.

The household consisted entirely of laymen except the two chaplains who may have been monks. It was with them that the abbot was closeted in the privacy of his chamber and chapel, for a chapel seems to have been an essential part of any of his houses, as with bishops. The household included some relatives: the abbot's mother and sister, the only two females, and two nephews who where students. The 'pages' who are mentioned frequently and sometimes got up to mischief were presumably boys or youths being trained or educated, apprentice squires as it were, being instructed in the ways of gentlemen.

Some aspects of the everyday arrangements may surprise: the self-sufficiency implied by the baking and brewing and the constant attention to what local prices might be, so that costs were no higher or where local purchases had to be made the best bargains were obtained. Illumination after dark was of course a major problem at the time, and the question of who was entitled to candles was an important matter, particularly for reading and writing, not easy by the light of a flickering oil torch. One obtains an insight into the porter's responsibilities, particularly who was excluded at the gate, especially bogus livery claimants and undesirable females and youths. Within the household gradations of status were marked by the amount and quality of fur on the livery gown. The English word for the whole body of the household was the *meiny*.

Abbot Walter had a special reason for wanting to cut a figure himself with suitably dressed squires among the '*grans seignors*' of Parliament since at this date it met in the polygonal chapter house of Westminster Abbey, recently rebuilt together with the abbey church by Henry III (1216-72). Abbot Walter was therefore in some sense the host to Parliament.

It is not necessary to follow this fascinating document further, for what is described is not significantly different from a lay household of this date. What is important to appreciate is that for most of his time in his peripatetic life the abbot was acting as head of this household and not acting as head of the abbey. The day-to-day running of the abbey — presiding over daily chapter, seeing that the divine offices were held at the proper time and so on — rested with the prior and his lieutenants. There was a long list of obedientaries all looking towards the prior rather than the abbot for direction. The abbot did not wash his hands of abbey affairs: the relationship was more like that of chairman and managing director of a firm.

The abbot in national affairs

As a monk at St Albans, Matthew Paris (1200-59) could cast his eye over the monastic world paying particular attention to the appointment of bishops and abbots, but his interests extended over much of Europe and the east Mediterranean area. Between 1236 and 1259, the year that Paris died, we have a great deal of information about the activities of abbots and bishops. Bishops were more important; an abbot might be elevated to a bishopric but never the other way round. On the whole bishops were the leaders in national affairs, at least among the clergy. Nevertheless it is clear that the leading Benedictine abbots of Bury St Edmunds, St Albans and Westminster played a considerable part on the national stage, and that the abbot of Westminster because of his location beside the Palace of Westminster might be regarded as leader (Giles, 1852, iii, 20, 92, 289). In 1251 the abbot of Westminster arrived from Rome having been appointed the Pope's chaplain, which made a great impression (Giles, ii, 444).

Bishops, abbots and priors had been summoned to the Great Council that advised the king from even before the Norman Conquest, that is to the *Witangemot* as it was called in late Saxon times (Powell and Wallis, 1968). It was a fairly haphazard business right up to the fourteenth century. The problem was that there were several hundred abbots and priors but only 21 bishops in England and Wales; the abbots outnumbered the bishops in Parliament, the successor to the great Council, right up to the Dissolution when the abbots of course disappear altogether.

White as well as black abbots Benedictine, Augustinian and Cistercian, sat in the House of Lords in the thirteenth century in for example the Parliament of 1295 (Powell and Wallis, 225) but the abbatial list, those who received a summons, stabilised in the fourteenth century; in 1327 19 abbots, all black, 16 Benedictine and three Augustinian, attended. By the reign of Henry IV (1399-1413) the list had become fixed. At the beginning of Henry VIII's reign (1509) the lords spiritual consisted of two archbishops, 19 bishops and 28 abbots. By 1536 at the beginning of the Dissolution 31 out of 52 spiritual peers were abbots.

It is sometimes thought that being 'mitred' automatically conferred Parliamentary status on an abbot. The conferment of mitre, crozier, ring, pectoral cross and glove was a papal act, giving quasi-episcopal status, but there was a number of 'mitred' abbots who did not receive a summons to the House of Lords, and not all those were mitred. The selection for the final list seems to have been mainly on seniority so they were largely from pre-Conquest foundations; 15 of them had had military service imposed on them by William I (Chew, 1932, 5), so enjoyed a special relationship to the Crown. The list of Parliamentary abbots reads as follows: Abingdon, St Albans, Bardney, Battle, Bury St Edmunds, Burton, Canterbury (St Augustines), Cirencester (Augustinian), Colchester, Coventry Crowland, Evesham, Glastonbury, Gloucester, St Benet's of Holme, Hyde, Malmesbury, Peterborough, Ramsey, Reading, Selby, Shrewsbury, Tavistock, Tewkesbury, Thorney, Waltham (Augustinian), Westminster (and Prior), Winchcombe, and York (St Marys). In addition the Knights Hospitallers' house of St John of Jerusalem in London was represented by its prior.

The feature that strikes one about the list is the lack of any Cistercian, Carthusian or Friar representation, and of the very numerous Augustinian houses in the country only two were summoned. The great Cistercian monasteries like Fountains, Rievaulx and Tintern were not represented and no abbey north of York and Selby had a seat. Attendance at Westminster was quite a burden (even if the distance was not as far as Cîteaux) and so there was probably little resentment felt by the northern abbots at their exclusion.

The loss of 31 abbots at the Dissolution of the monasteries greatly reduced the representation of the lords spiritual in the House of Lords, although six more bishoprics were created. Abbots now vanished from the scene; most went peaceably but three parliamentary abbots from Glastonbury, Reading and Colchester were hanged.

London

There were at least three reasons why an abbot or monastery might need property in London: as an investment from rent, as an office conducting business and providing accommodation for its agents, and lastly as a residence for the head of house. Property could of course be acquired by gift, purchase, bequest or merely rented.

With the bishops the use of a London property was primarily as a residence, no doubt valuable during Parliamentary sessions; we have a surviving example at Lambeth Palace (M.W. Thompson, 1998). No doubt some of the abbots' houses in London served the same purpose. Thus John Stow's 'great house' of the abbot of Ramsey abbey in Beech Lane was surely primarily a residence. In Appendix IV I have separated those houses where the abbot or prior had Parliamentary duties from the fourteenth century and those that did not. For the first category the residential aspect of the house was perhaps most important, while for the second business was perhaps the main consideration. For example the 'large messuage' belonging to the French house of Fécamp in Normandy situated by the riverside was surely primarily used for commerce.

John Schofield has most kindly drawn my attention to several other abbots' houses not included in his book (Schofield, 1995). While the list is not complete (it never can be), it is surprising that no record or memory seems to have survived into the later Middle Ages of the Cistercian properties that Donkin (1978) identified in the capital. Perhaps they were offices connected with the wool trade that were no longer needed or had some other commercial function that had lapsed. Only one Cistercian property in London features in the list in Appendix IV, Waverley in Surrey, the earliest Cistercian house in the country, which remained fairly small but important. The list does not include monastic foundations actually situated in or near London which have been the subject of a valuable study and upon which exploration continues (Sloane, 1999, particularly fig. 1 showing 25 sites).

Unlike bishops' houses, which were largely found between London and Westminster particularly on the river frontage of the left bank, there is no definite concentration of abbots' houses in London. The only suggestion of a cluster is around the bridge on the south bank at Southwark.

5 The monastic precinct

The monastic precinct

The abbot of St Edmunds . . . to the derision of all, setting a pernicious example
to the monks, and to the injury of the Holy order, violated every vow, and also
assumed the cross . . .
Matthew Paris, 1250 (Giles, 1852, ii, 330).

The abbot of Bury St Edmunds abbey in 1250 had touched on a very sensitive area in
medieval society: the function of one class of society was fighting, another of praying and
a third of physical work. There were of course exceptions like the military Orders, so that
Templars and Hospitallers in their struggle with the infidels in the Levant could and did
erect large castles in their sacred crusade to recover Jerusalem. At home however the
matter was clear: the clergy had no business to take up arms or fortify their premises, and
with the religious, the regular clergy, who had taken vows, it was a serious sin to do so. By
signing up for a crusade the abbot of St Edmunds was in flagrant breach of the rules.

The monks therefore were placed at a disadvantage, living as they did in an intensely
violent society racked by social unrest (M.W. Thompson, 1998). Blatant military
fortification was not possible except when the enemy was regarded as alien, as at Ewenny
Priory Glamorgan, where the gate and precinct of the convent are strongly fortified. A
much more lenient view was taken in the case of the secular clergy: a comparison between
the steps taken by the bishops on the one hand and the abbots on the other to protect
themselves in a world where the church was not in as strong a position in popular
affections as it had been is illuminating.

Before making such comparisons a word about attacks on monasteries should be said.
In the Midlands there were attacks from the 1220s at Dunstable, Bromley, Burton
(Crossley, 1949, 98), and at Bury St Edmunds in 1264 (Yates, 1843, 125). These are merely
ones that have come to my attention. No doubt the civil wars at the end of Henry III's
reign nourished disorders from which time the licences to crenellate start. Attacks became
common in the early fourteenth century: in Bury St Edmunds in 1305 (Yates, 1893, 128),
and in 1313 Thetford was invaded by the mob and several people were killed at the altar
(Dymond, 1995, 2). The chronicles of St Albans and Bury St Edmunds record very
serious violence in 1326-7 at the former when the abbey itself and its manors were
attacked and damaged, and at Bury St Edmunds in 1327-8 the abbey and manors were
attacked and the abbot abducted. The disturbing feature of the rioting was that it
encompassed both the abbey itself and its manors, 22 of which suffered some damage
mainly by theft of livestock. The urban risings could of course raise a much larger force
than purely rural movements. The reader will know about the 1381 and 1450 risings, the
latter not having the East Anglian nor perhaps such an anti-monastic aspect.

The attacks at the monastic boroughs, that is where the town was an adjunct of a large monastery within it, like Bury St Edmunds and St Albans, were very widespread in 1326-7 and 1381 and not confined to East Anglia but extended to the Midlands and Home Counties. The matter has been discussed by David Knowles in 1966 (vol. ii, 264-9) who named other Benedictine abbeys which suffered serious disturbances and damage. The grievances of the peasants on the one hand and the burgesses on the other were not the same, although the latter tended to exploit the problems of the former and provided the leadership.

Powell (1895, 62) in his accounts of events in 1381 Norfolk, Suffolk and Cambridgeshire wrote:

> Many of the minor clergy . . . were eager partisans in the insurrection . . . and did not shrink from dyeing their hands in blood . . . the regular clergy who inhabited the larger religious houses had evidently made themselves the object of the intense hatred of the common people, and were persistently attacked during the rising.

Apart from monks and lawyers probably the worst victims of 'beheadings' (*decollata*) were the 'Flemings'. The mob had strong prejudices but evidently was not certain about its objectives, although it is clear that it was not anti-clerical *per se*.

Monastic licences to crenellate

A licence to crenellate (make battlements), a royal authorisation from Chancery recorded on the back of the Patent Rolls, started to be issued in the second half of the thirteenth century. The licences have disappeared and what survives is the record entry on the back of the Patent Roll. They were issued to laity and clergy alike. While not all were for full-scale military works, probably indeed only a minority, they are very valuable for dating construction of fortified buildings. For clerical licences a list of those issued to bishops will be found in M.W. Thompson, 1998, 167-8, while a list of abbots' licences will be found in Appendix V. A comparison of the two is extremely interesting.

Several points at once stand out. The monastic licences start later (1293) and end abruptly in 1399 since the 1410 licence is merely a repeat of the earlier one. Secondly, only a very small proportion of the total number of religious houses acquired licences; among bishops it was common. The licensed abbeys were mainly Benedictine, some Augustinian and one or two Premonstratensian or Cistercian. As we might expect the severer Orders were less keen on licensing; the Carthusians had none.

The most striking difference between the two is the rarity of licensing for monastic manors, as opposed to the abbey buildings themselves. There are only five monastic licences for manors, all in the north-west of England: Piel of Foudray, Lancashire, in 1327; Wolsty 'castle', Cumberland on the Solway Firth in 1348; Ince, Little Sutton and Saighton Grange in Cheshire in 1399. The first two to judge by their remains were virtually castles and strongly fortified, while the three Cheshire licences were issued when the Owain

Glyndwr's Welsh rising was just starting in the adjoining county (Glyndwr was a native of Clwyd). The inference is clear: a licence for defence of a monastic manor was permissible when there was a perceived alien threat (Scottish or Welsh in these cases) but otherwise could not be considered socially acceptable. It illustrates the constraints imposed on the religious orders, as opposed to the bishops who seem to have been free to licence their manor buildings as they wished.

Turning now to the abbey buildings themselves, what was the nature of the work that the licence permitted? Why indeed was licensing necessary? The entries are laconic and probably euphemistic because of protocol. In 1318 St Mary's York was allowed to enclose the monastery with a wall but it was not to be more than 16ft (5m) high, rather less than a full military height. Other entries refer to walling, adding chambers or houses, or simply 'crenellating' the church and so on. There are significant cases like Peterborough, Canterbury St Augustines, or Thornton Abbey, Lincolnshire, which refer to the gatehouse and the building that survives. References to crenellating the belfry at Langley, Drax, Shaftesbury are puzzling. The Norman tower gate at Bury St Edmunds presumably was also a belfry, and it perhaps is to this kind of belfry that the entries refer. The entries speak of building houses over, beside or in front of gatehouses, and the intention may have been to provide further accommodation so that there could be manning by something more than a single porter. The surviving gatehouses certainly suggest a desire for more accommodation.

Why did the licences for monastic houses stop so abruptly at the end of the fourteenth century when they continued for bishops and laymen up to the Reformation and even beyond? There must always have been doubt whether these decidedly unmilitary gatehouses required a licence for their construction. Their purpose was to overawe a mob, creating a place for negotiation, not to resist attack. When crenellation was becoming a form for decorative parapets on parish churches it was absurd to think that a battlemented top on a gatehouse made it a military building. There may also have been some falling-off in the especially anti-monastic threat, although large monastic gatehouses continued to be built right up to the time of the Dissolution of the monasteries.

Late medieval monastic gatehouses

A recent book on this subject (Morant, 1995) gives a wealth of valuable detail on these gatehouses, and the reader who wishes for typology, classification and architectural detail can refer to that book. Here the matter is treated in a different, more historical way.

Massive military gatehouses with a narrow opening flanked by projecting towers, usually with drawbridges in front and closed by a portcullis, were in use from the early thirteenth century in castles, town gates and other forms of lay fortification. These were clearly too overtly military to be suitable for monastic use. The monastic gatehouse derives from earlier forms relying on a square or rectangular tower often with corner turrets, a wide carriageway often flanked by a wicket or pedestrian doorway which can be repeated at the back (**frontispiece & 32**). This feature, so distinctive of monastic gatehouses, will be discussed below together with other matters such as sculpture.

*52 Battle abbey, Sussex, back view of gatehouse, licensed 1338. Cf. **frontispiece**. Note through-passage of wicket doors. A.E. Thompson*

53 Peterborough abbey, early thirteenth-century gatehouse to abbot's house, seen from outside. Note sculptured figures. A.E. Thompson

54 Peterborough abbey, outside of West gatehouse, licensed 1308. A.E. Thompson

William de Chireton, abbot of Evesham (1317-46) received a licence to crenellate in 1332, which led no doubt to what was recorded by the monastery's chronicler (Macray, 1863, 291-2):

> He made in addition a noble gateway to the abbey in the outer court towards the town with vaults, chapels and chambers disposed about it, neatly crenellated on top, with stone statues of the Blessed Virgin, St Egwin and our royal founders set within the centre, and another gate in Berton towards Merstow, well equipped, neatly crenellated on top . . .

Several points may be made about this description. The chronicler says nothing about the licence perhaps because he was ashamed of the house having to have one, unless he simply did not know. The 'great gate' (*magna porta*) seems to have been a late medieval invention, always on the outer perimeter of the precinct and usually facing the town. The neat battlements perhaps were partly symbolic: the monastery was prepared to stand up for its right against a crowd; it was their use, which made the licence desirable or necessary. The chapel was needed by the entering or leaving travellers like the chapel on a medieval bridge. No hall is mentioned but chambers sound like residential lodgings. The remains of the Evesham gatehouse are now incorporated into a later building and so are not suitable for illustration but compare **53**, **54** and **55** of Peterborough gatehouses.

55 Peterborough abbey, outside of West gatehouse showing earlier twelfth-century gate encased in 1308 in such a way as to allow a portcullis to be fitted. A.E. Thompson

56 Bury St Edmunds abbey, mid-fourteenth-century great gatehouse from outside. Note niches for sculpture, portcullis and battlements (restored). A.E. Thompson

The two gatehouses at the great Benedictine abbeys of St Albans and Bury St Edmunds have parallel histories, which throw much light on this subject. Both monasteries suffered severely in the rioting of 1326-8. At Bury St Edmunds an earlier gate (not the Norman bell tower) was burnt and much serious damage was done in the abbey precinct, with thieving in its manors and the notorious abduction of the abbot who was arrived off to the Brabant (Arnold, 1892, ii, 327-57). The large and very handsome gatehouse can be dated to the years following the *Depredatio*, as it is called (**56**). At St Albans the same unrest started earlier in 1326 leading also to extensive damage to abbey and manors (Riley, 1965, ii, 156-81). The abbey apparently did not have a great gate but Abbot Richard of Wallingford (1326-35) had a newly constructed almonry pulled down for the construction

57 St Albans abbey gatehouse, licensed 1357, outside view. Note wicket door. A.E. Thompson

of new great gate; the matter had become one of urgency. The construction was not satisfactory or incomplete since it fell down. The next abbot, Thomas de la Mare, who had a very long period of office, 1349-96, obtained a licence in 1357 after which the present gatehouse was built. Abbot Thomas not only built the gate but also was able to watch it in action in 1381 (**57 & 58**). For an account of Abbot Thomas see Knowles (1966, iii, 39-48).

So both abbeys had very substantial gatehouses by 1381 at the time of the rising. The initial crowd at the gate of Bury in 1327 had been estimated at 3000, and subsequently some 20,000 people were said to have been involved in the unrest. Allowing for medieval exaggeration we are still dealing with large numbers. In 1381 at St Albans the initial march with banners on the gatehouse was estimated to have consisted of 2000 people, and the later return (the trouble went on for several days) at 1500 people. It is not surprising that the Prior and some monks wished to make a run to the manors. The mob on arriving had opened the abbot's prison and released the prisoners except for one who for reasons unknown they beheaded on the site. Their demands were for charters of liberties, which they believed were being concealed from them. We will not discuss the letter from the king or the extent to which London agitators and reinforcements played in the events. Abbot Thomas was a brave and shrewd man who realised that safety lay in the sanctity of the abbey; the abbot at Bury St Edmunds had been abducted from a manor in 1328, and in 1381 the Prior was beheaded when in a manor. His was among several heads displayed at Bury.

The gatehouse at St Albans was central to events and presumably where negotiations took place. Towards the end, when the patience of the mob was almost exhausted and

58 St Albans abbey gatehouse from inside looking through gateway and wicket. In 1381 there were several hundred rioters outside. A.E. Thompson

59 *Pentney, Norfolk. The great fourteenth-century gatehouse stands in lonely isolation as the Augustinian priory to which it led has disappeared.* A.E. Thompson

60 *Ely priory, great gatehouse, front view.* A.E. Thompson

61 Ely priory, great gatehouse, back view. A.E. Thompson

before assistance arrived, the crowd 'out of sheer malice' threatened to demolish the whole new gatehouse '*si quisquam vellet percutere primum ictum*' ('if anyone is willing to strike the first blow') (Riley, 1965, ii, 312). No one was. The words ring down the years; the success of the new gatehouse at St Albans must have made a deep impression on other abbots.

At Bury St Edmunds the troubles were severe enough to judge by the beheading of the prior (the abbot was in Nottingham at the time). The vigorous steps taken by the bishop of Norwich to put down the disturbances meant the troubles were not as prolonged as in 1327-8. The abbey suffered less and the magnificent gatehouse came through it unscathed so far as we can tell.

Powell (1895, 34) found that in the three weeks in which the trouble lasted in June-July, 1381, the priories of Bromholm, Binham and Carrow were forced to give up their court rolls to be publicly burnt. West Dereham abbey was attacked and ransacked, as were Corpus Christi College and Barnwell Priory at Cambridge. A night attack by 400 rebels on St Benet's at Holm in the Broads was repulsed after severe fighting and an attack on Ramsey in the Fens probably had the same result. Other large Benedictine abbeys like Ely or Peterborough seem to have escaped.

The lesson of the success of the gatehouse at St Albans appears to been learnt at the large Augustinian abbey of Thornton in North Lincolnshire where a licence was obtained in 1382 specifically referring to the great gatehouse which was then rebuilt in the form we see it today (**62 & 63**). A second licence was obtained in 1389 couched in more general

62 Thornton abbey, Lincolnshire, back of great gatehouse, licensed 1382. Note the bow window.
   A.E. Thompson

terms and was perhaps intended to authorise the works required for the great ditch and high wall that surround the abbey precinct. The barbican projecting from the front, which gives the gatehouse a decidedly military look, is a later addition although after what lapse of time it is not possible to say. This is the largest of the monastic gatehouses and one of the best preserved. How the very ample accommodation inside was meant to be used has been a matter of controversy. That the abbot occupied it is very unlikely, although the fireplace and bow window at first-floor level with further chambers above all linked to passages in a sort of curtain wall certainly suggest its use by an important official rather than as a court room (**64** shows Emery's plans at different floor levels). One leaf of the great two-leaf gate survives and there are groves for a portcullis. Without doubt it is a remarkable structure.

63 Thornton abbey, outside view of great gatehouse. Note surviving sculpture including crowning of Virgin in centre. Brick barbican is a later addition. A.E. Thompson

The west gate at Peterborough, licensed in 1308, has a twelfth-century gateway that was encased at the later date in such a way as to create grooves for a portcullis (*see* **55**). The gatehouse at Bury St Edmunds had a provision for a portcullis (*see* **56**). So the monastic gatehouses were not entirely without means for military-style closure.

The whole function of the monastic great gate of this date was designed to make the maximum impression on someone approaching it from the outside so that the back can be different from the front as for example at St John's gate at Colchester which has panelled decoration on the outside only (*see* **16**). Many of the gatehouses bear sculpture on the outside although they have usually lost it since the Reformation. When the niches on the great gate at Bury St Edmunds held their original sculpture it must have been an

64 *Thornton abbey gatehouse, plans at three floor levels. Note the spacious accommodation, wall passages, provision for portcullis and later barbican.* A. Emery, *Greater Medieval Houses of England and Wales*, 2, fig. 83

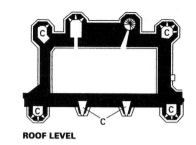

ROOF LEVEL

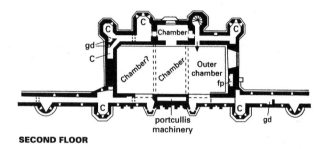

SECOND FLOOR

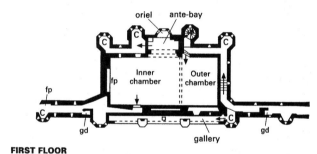

FIRST FLOOR

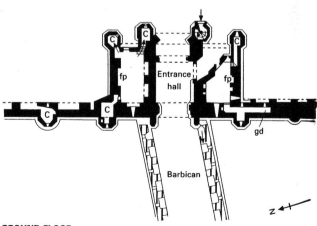

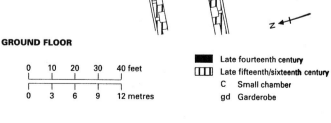

GROUND FLOOR

| 0 | 10 | 20 | 30 | 40 feet |
| 0 | 3 | 6 | 9 | 12 metres |

■ Late fourteenth century
▥ Late fifteenth/sixteenth century
C Small chamber
gd Garderobe

119

Drawn by G.Wild.   Engraved by G.Hollis.

65 (left) Canterbury, St Augustine's abbey, great gate, licensed 1308, an early example

66 (above) Colchester, St Johns fifteenth-century gatehouse. Note decorative flushwork.
A.E. Thompson

67 Bridlington priory, Yorkshire, great gate from outside, licensed 1388, much rebuilt.
   A.E. Thompson

impressive sight. At Thornton (**63**) three figures survive (now replaced by fibreglass so the originals are protected from the weather): the Virgin being crowned in the middle, with St John and possibly St Augustine on either side (it was an Augustinian house). At Evesham it may be remembered that the Virgin, tutelary saint and royal founders were displayed. An approaching mob might well hesitate in the face of the Virgin or even Christ in majesty and tutelary saints, since however disorganised such a body might be at this date its members would regard themselves as Christians.

   This brings us to the wicket gate, that is a small pedestrian door on one side or in late examples occasionally on both sides of the main vehicular carriageway. Occasionally the pedestrian passage passed right through so there was a wicket in the back of the gatehouse

*68 St Osyths priory, Essex, great gate of c.1500 from outside. Compare its flushwork with that of Colchester, St Johns in **66**.* A.E. Thompson

(discussed in Morant, 1995). The wicket was evidently to exercise extra control at certain times as with a Cambridge college, the wicket alone being used after dark or when the college plate was on display. It needs no emphasis that with a crowd of several hundred outside a sudden surge would bring it into the monastic court if the vehicular passage was open, but if closed essential ingress and egress could take place or negotiations with a hostile crowd could be made through the wicket. This may well be what happened in June 1381 (**58**) at St Albans.

The last monastic gatehouse for which there is a licence, the Augustinian house at Bridlington, licensed in 1388 (**67**, rebuilt above), did not bring to an end the construction of large monastic gatehouses; indeed some of the finest were built between then and the Reformation, of which two are illustrated here, St John's at Colchester and St Osyth also in Essex (**65 & 68**). Both are decorated on the outside with elaborate flushwork and are around the same date, that is *c.*1500, St Osyth being the finer of the two. It would be a bold man who suggested that it was not expected to have at least some protective function for the monastery that it shielded. The immensely elaborate pattern of heraldic shields over the gate at Butley Priory, Suffolk, of local gentry has allowed a relatively early fourteenth-century date to be given to the building, a fair reminder that the ornamental aspect of these buildings counted from the beginning (Myers, 1933). The fine traceried windows leave one in no doubt that this was not a military building, although perhaps the bearers of the heraldry in the shields were prepared to offer protection to the monastery (**69 & 70**). The ground plan with its projecting wings is unusual and a little more military than one might have expected.

Drawn & Engraved by John Coney

Butley Priory. Suffolk.

69 Butley Priory, Suffolk. Early nineteenth-century view of gatehouse from outside. Note great display of heraldry over gateway and traceried windows above. Coney

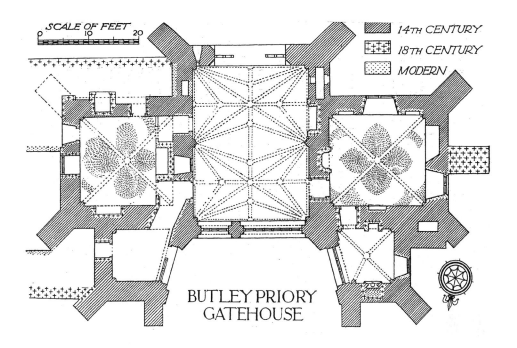

SCALE OF FEET
0   10   20

14TH CENTURY
18TH CENTURY
MODERN

BUTLEY PRIORY
GATEHOUSE

70 *Butley Priory, Suffolk. Plan of ground floor of early fourteenth-century gatehouse. Note finely vaulted passage and chambers projecting on either side of entry.* Caroe and Myers, *Archaeological Journal* 90

The influence of monastic gatehouses on other collegiate buildings was very great. At Cambridge we need only compare the innocuous entry at Pembroke College (founded 1347) with fifteenth-century foundations like Queen's or St John's colleges to see the point. It affected lay domestic architecture also since the great gatehouse, based on a monastic rather than a military style, became the normal entry to the courtyards of fifteenth-century and early Tudor houses.

There is an analogy with machicolations, the projections on the outer face of fortified walls so constructed that they created an opening for dropping missiles down the face of the wall onto the enemy, which were a functional construction when they became normal in the fourteenth century. They so enhanced the appearance of the building that they were kept as an ornamental feature for long afterwards; it is only when there is no hole that one can be certain that they have no practical use and are purely ornamental. Similarly with monastic gatehouses, which no doubt had an ornamental element in them from the beginning, it is impossible to say at what point they became entirely ornamental if indeed they ever did, for there is no definite criterion as with machicolations to clearly mark this point.

6 Conclusion

Conclusion

In our modern sceptical and hedonistic world the general reader finds monachism quite opposed in every area to the principles on which his own life is founded. The monk is contemptuous of this world in his certainty of a better one to come and rejoices in the prospect of death knowing of the following union with God. He rejects personal comfort, indeed welcoming discomfort as a test of fitness for this future, and perhaps even more important rejecting private property for the same reason (individual property of course, not for the establishment in which he lived). Without the faith from which this flowed we find any fellow feeling hard to achieve, but whatever the shortcomings of institutionalised monachism, and they were many, even the most hardened atheist must admire the effort made to accomplish its aims. In the Middle Ages it was regarded as the highest form of aspiration; unless the effort is made to understand this the period will remain a meaningless jumble, however serious the student may be in pursing his studies of this period.

In this book four themes have been chosen to illustrate some aspects of what appears a rather alien subject. It is not purely historical, nor purely architectural, nor indeed archaeological, although it borrows features from all three. Taken in isolation these methods can be rather arid, but suitably mixed something more satisfactory, at least to the author's mind, can emerge.

Four aspects of monachism have been touched upon. The origins in upper Egypt are fundamental to its understanding; the transition from eremitism to cenobitism; a compromise between an unachievable ideal and a real world that imposed certain conditions in order to fulfil part at least of what was intended. Pachomius is known from what he did rather than what he believed. No one can doubt his faith but he did not take up the pen to tell us what it was, for he was an organiser, even (dare one say it) an 'administrator'. So far as we know he had no experience of Essenes or other Jewish communities, the *koinonia* that he created owed more to his experience in the Roman army than to any civilian communities, other than his experience of Egyptian village life along the Nile.

Apart from the communities that he created in the Thebaid in Upper Egypt much interest must surround the diffusion from this area into the numerous Christian communities in the Roman Empire. No doubt the political unity over the area assisted this but monachism spread beyond into Ethiopia and the Celtic areas at the other extreme. Diffusion is a subject of great interest to anthropologists and archaeologists but the writer cannot pretend to have a full knowledge or understanding of how this happened.

The second subject discussed was the cloister, its origins and development, now more a matter of architectural history. It is a feature that sharply distinguishes western monasticism from eastern, not only in the buildings but also in the sort of ethos it creates within the monastery. On the question of whether it was designed or simply hit upon a middle position is adopted: it no doubt had elements of both. The instability of the function of the west range was one of the points that most evidently emerged, so clearly demonstrated when the reforming Orders, notably the Cistercians, were adapting the cloister to their own particular requirements. Although only the cloisters of the two main Orders were considered, the contrast was very striking — Cistercians adapting the existing cloister and the Carthusians breaking almost completely with the traditional form to meet their own very exacting requirements. The adaptations of the mendicant Orders of friars again vividly illustrate their very different relationship with the laity. Something of a nuisance for monks, for friars the cultivation, not to say wooing, of the laity was central to their duties. The cloister was still an essential element in monastic life right up to the Dissolution even if some of the buildings around it were on their last legs. Where monasteries continued in use as in France it was the demands of the new style of Classical architecture that rendered the Gothic cloister unnecessary.

The St Gall plan was discussed, not from the point of view of the church which has perhaps received too much attention, but from the point of view of the cloister and its relationship to the estate buildings that almost completely surround it. Although in so many ways fully mature, the absentee from the plan is the chapter house, so essential an element in later monastic life. The buildings on the north side of the church were not normal in later monasteries and the abbot's house was of special interest in view of the next chapter where the abbot's position in the monastery was the subject. It is a remarkable building subdivided at both floor levels with its own heating arrangements and verandahs on both long sides, and of course its own kitchen, bathhouse and latrines. This raised the whole question of why the abbot was living outside the cloister and how this could be reconciled with the decisions of the synods of Aachen on where the abbot ought to be living.

The first two chapters had strayed geographically over a large area but the remaining three chapters were confined largely to England, only very occasionally going outside it. Indeed the last chapter became even more restricted to southern or eastern England! The third topic was the abbot, first in the monastery, and then outside it, making particular comparison with medieval bishops dealt with elsewhere (M. Thompson, 1998).

The first task was to establish where the abbots were living in the cloister, which could be inferred from where they emerged in the fourteenth century, either from the west range (Benedictine, Augustinian) or the east range (Cistercian). The exceptions to the norm were of great interest, where the Orders may have influenced each other. The next point to cover was how the abbots or priors lived when they emerged from the cloister, and their houses were briefly described, or at all events a sample of them. In describing the contraction in use of the cloister in the previous chapter reference had already been made to the central part played by the abbot's or prior's hall for the whole body of the religious in the century before the Dissolution.

Still on this theme the situation of the abbot outside the monastery was discussed. The importance of the manors where they had residences was referred to although the numbers of these, which must have run into hundreds, did not allow any serious detail.

Very few indeed survive. The extraordinarily interesting instructions for the household of Walter of Wenlock abbot of Westminster abbey from 1295 translated in Appendix III were discussed. It fits in very well with the picture of a peripatetic abbot we have from his itinerary, apart from a vivid picture of the whole system of hall-and-chamber culture when it was in full swing. The abbot's other activities particularly in Parliament and London were briefly discussed; the abbots played a very important part in national affairs and normally outnumbered the bishops in the House of Lords up to the Dissolution, when of course they disappeared.

The last theme in the final chapter touched on the protection of the precinct in the troubled period of the fourteenth century. The medieval disapproval of monks fortifying monasteries except where there was a very self-evident danger, normally from an alien enemy, meant that the fortification undertaken by lay landowners with towers and walls was not open to them. The licences to crenellate issued in some profusion to lay landowners for this purpose were very rarely issued to the abbots for their manors and only when there was self-evident danger. The licences issued for the monasteries themselves were few in number and hardly suggest a very bold form of fortification. The chief element was the great gatehouse with living accommodation inside and armed with little more than a portcullis, not designed to stand a siege but to overawe a mob, an assertion of monastic authority as it were. They were probably quite often put to the test, certainly at St Albans and probably at Bury St Edmunds. Monastic gatehouse building reached a climax in 1382 at Thornton Abbey, Lincolnshire after the 1381 rising. Large gatehouses continued to be built into the next century although licences were no longer issued for them. The hostility towards the monks so apparent in East Anglia in the fourteenth century may well have significantly declined in the next century.

We have followed the monks in these few brief essays, from their first coming into existence in the final period of the Roman Empire to the climax of monachism in twelfth-century France up to the time when there was open hostility to them. Their shortness may commend itself to the reader in a field where brevity is at a premium, and in a subject that is perhaps best taken in small doses.

Appendix I
Situation of the abbot

Original situation of abbot or prior in the cloister inferred from later abbot/prior's houses in published plans or specific references. An asterisk means the final position of the abbot's house is misleading as to original position.

In the west or cellarer's range

Benedictine
Bardney Abbey, Lincs.
Battle Abbey, Sussex
Binham Priory, Norfolk
Canterbury, St Augustines Abbey
Glastonbury Abbey, Somerset
Gloucester Abbey
Muchelney Abbey, Somerset
Peterbourough Abbey, Northants.
Westminster Abbey

Cluniac
Castle Acre Priory, Norfolk
Monk Bretton Priory, Yorks. (later Benedictine)
Thetford Priory, Norfolk

Augustinian Canons
Anglesey Priory, Cambs.
Barnwell Priory, Cambs.
Bradenstoke Priory, Wilts.
Bristol abbey, Glos.
Butley Priory, Suffolk
Dover Priory, Kent
Dunstable Priory, Beds.
Great Bricett Priory, Suffolk
?Haugmond Abbey, Shopshire. Abbot's later lodging south of refectory
Lacock Abbey, Wilts (Cannonesses) N. cloister

Lanercrost Priory, Cumb.
Leicester, St Mary de Pre Abbey
Lilleshall Abbey, Shropshire
Michelham Priory, Sussex
Newark Priory, Surrey
Norton Abbey, Cheshire
St Osyth Priory, Essex
Shilbred Priory, Sussex
?Thornton Abbey, Lincs.
Wigmore Abbey, Heref.

Premonstratensian Canons
Bayham Abbey, Sussex
Eggleston abbey, Yorks.
Leiston Abbey, Suffolk
?Shap Abbey, Westmoreland
St Radegunds Abbey, nr Dover, Kent

Gilbertine
Watton Priory, Yorks. (nuns and canons)

Tironian
Arbroath Abbey, Forfarshire

⋆Cistercian
Forde Abbey, Dorset, N. cloister
Robertsbridge, Sussex

In the east (dormitory) range and moved eastwards

Cistercian
Byland Abbey, Yorks.
Croxden Abbey, Staffs.
Fountains Abbey, Yorks.
Furness Abbey, Lancs.
Jervaulx Abbey, Yorks.
Kirkstall Abbey, Yorks.
Melrose Abbey, Roxburgh. North cloister
Neath Abbey, W. Glamorgan. South of refectory
Netley Abbey, Hants.
Quarr Abbey, Isle of Wight
Rievaulx Abbey, Yorks.
Roche Abbey, Yorks.

Thame Park Abbey, Oxon.
Tintern Abbey, Monmouthshire. N. cloister
Valle Crucis Abbey, Clwyd

★Benedictine
Bury St Edmunds, Suffolk. N. Cloister.
Finchale Priory, Durham
Lindisfarne Priory, Northumberland
Milton Abbey, Dorset. N. cloister
Tynemouth Priory, Northumberland
York, St Mary's Abbey?

★Cluniac
Much Wenlock Priory, Shropshire

★Augustinian Canons
Bolton Abbey, Yorks. (originally *W. range*)
?Guisborough Priory, Yorks.
Ixworth Priory, Suffolk
Kirkham Priory, Yorks.
Lesnes Abbey, Kent. N. cloister
?Oxford, St Frideswide Priory

Appendix II
Rural houses

A sample of rural houses of abbots and priors. These are more or less random with several examples taken from Platt's book on medieval monastic granges (1969). Monastic manor houses or granges with suitable accommodation for head of houses must have run well into four figures during the Middle Ages.

Abingdon Abbey:
Charney Bassett, Berks. Stone buildings exist (Platt, 197-8)
Sutton Courtenay, Berks. Hall and chamber (Platt, 236-7)

Bristol Augustinian Priory:
Ashleworth, Glos. Fifteenth-century house survives (Platt, 187-8)

Bury St Edmunds Abbey:
Chevington, Suffolk. Abbot seized by rebels here in 1328 and taken to London and then the Continent
Elmswell, Suffolk. Henry VI entertained here. There is a large moated area adjoining the church
Mildenhall, Suffolk

Canterbury St Augustine's Abbey:
Minster in Thanet where chapel, hall etc. survive (Platt, 18-19, 217-19)
Salmstone, Kent. Chapel and hall (Platt, 231-2)

Chester St Werburgh's Abbey:
Ince, Cheshire. Licensed 1399. Part of a late fifteenth-century hall in ruin with windows and a second building at right angles survive (Emery, 2000, ii, 551-3)
Little Sutton, Cheshire. Licensed 1399. Nothing survives
Saighton, Cheshire. Licensed 1399. A large residential gatehouse of *c.*1490 survives attached to nineteenth-century building (Emery, 2000, ii, 569-71)

Furness, Abbey:
Piel of Foudray, Lancs. Licensed 1327. A tower within a curtain on an island as shown on Bucks view (Emery, 1996, i 240)

Glastonbury Abbey:

Meare, Somerset. Described in a survey of 1539: 'The Manner of Mere . . . of an auncynt buylding, having a fayre large hall, thone halfe whereof is covered with lead and thither withslate, with viii fayre chambers, a proper chapel, with kytchyn buttery and pantrye, and all other house of office very necessary. Fynally the house is fitt for a man of worship.' (Dugdale, I, 10)

Sharpham, nr Glastonbury. Abbot Whiting arrested there in 1539 before his trial and execution (Dugdale, i, 10)

Holmcultram Abbey:

Wolstey Castle, Cumb. Licensed 1348. On Solway Firth and later called a castle. Rectangular moat and lower parts of walls survive.

Reading Abbey:

Bere Court, nr Pangbourne, Berks. (Dugdale, 4, 33)
Cholsey, nr Wallingford, Berks. (Dugdale, 4, 33)

Westminster Abbey:

Mainly extracted from Harvey (1965) although to judge by the Itinerary it is incomplete. The main residences have been marked with an asterisk.
Bourton-on-the Hill, Glos.
Chippenham, Bucks.
*Chelsea, La Neyte. This, the abbot's most favoured residence, has disappeared without trace but the site was located by Rutton (1910)
* Claygate, Surrey
*Denham, Middx.
Eye, Middx.
*Islip, Oxon.
*Laleham, Middx.
Paddington
*Pershore,Worcs.
Pyrford, Surrey
Staines, Middx.
*Sutton-under-Brailes, Glos.
Todenham, Glos.

Worcester Priory:

Three manor houses, all very close to Worcester, where Prior William More (1518-35) spent most of his time (Fegan, 1914)
*Battenhall *(Batnall)*, SE of Worcester on outskirts. Moated area survives
*Crowle, Worcs. 5 miles E of the city
*Grimley, Worcs. 4 miles N of city

Appendix III
Abbot Walter's household

The household of Abbot Walter of Westminster (1283-1307)

The text that follows is a translation of the French in the transcript made by E.H. Pearce of the original document (muniment 24504, pp.99-104) which he published in 1920 (pp106-12) subsequently republished by Barbara Harvey under the title of *Household Ordinances* (1965, 4-6, 241-51). She discusses it at length in her book publishing writs and other documents issued by Abbot Walter of Wenlock and gives the date of 1295 to it. I have split the continuous text into paragraphs.

Walter by the grace of God Abbot of Westminster greets all his faithful servants. As it is necessary that each household member must follow a certain order for the maintenance of his household and its dignity we will and command that the order set out below be in force in all parts of our household.

First that we have specific receivers of our total cash from the bailiffs and reeves of all our lands, and they make records (*tayles*) of every receipt by the bailiffs and reeves for themselves. Thus there may be no main payment in future from the manorial accounts outside the records of the aforementioned receivers. Further these receivers make no payment without our written authority. And the guardians of our household take from the receivers such gross sums of money as may be necessary for the requirements of our household as seems most to our advantage. And that the chief receivers will make record of each payment made to the guardians of our household that so much has been received for its expenses, and that by their record it was a reasonable charge on their account. The expenses of the household will be audited before its officers each night in the presence of the steward (*seneschal*) of the household, which will cover all expenses both of the chamber and of the household. And if it happens that the Steward is at any time away with our permission or by our command then the roll of the household will be closed under his seal until he returns, and its expenses will not be entered before officers on a roll by themselves. On his return these expenses will be examined and entered in the principal roll. So that nothing may be entered on the principal roll in the Steward's absence it will be sealed each night after the audit with his seal.

Further we will and command that by the advice of stewards of our lands and our household the supplies are obtained from the fields and manors where we are intending to stay, according to what may be most to our dignity and profit. Also we wish that our Steward of lands carries out his office beyond his duty and that he has understood from ourselves the orders about the manors and that all the bailiffs and reeves have understood them and that his writs and instructions are received and performed according to his requirement in all matters that touch our dignity and repute. When he comes to our household he shall be received with three horses and his clerk and three servants during their stay and that he shall be honoured next to us. The steward of the household summons his accounts and shows him the state of the supplies and stores and of the treasure they hold. In this way there may be agreement about the ordering of necessary provisions and that if anything has to be put right where the body (*meisnee*) will be then it is done before their arrival, and this should be done as befits our honour and the good order of the household.

Next we will that the steward of our household has full charge within in all matters that bring profit and enhance our honour, and that its members (*meisnee*) are conversant and responsive to this. Further that officers keep and follow his authority and everything relating to their duties is duly recorded in indentures agreed with the steward, so that they be responsible by these documents for what they do and intend. All officers will come to the audit each night and in the presence of all straightly enquire into any irregularity, which can be put right in this way. First they can be hold to account and beaten for two minor misdemeanours, and if found culpable of offences a third time may be discharged by the steward and if it is a grave misdemeanour with which they are charged will be summarily dismissed. The steward should see that reparation is made to us for these offences so that we do not suffer loss. And we forbid that those who will be dismissed by the steward for these offences should return to our service by reconciliation.

And that the bailiffs and reeves will furnish by writ of the steward of our household for its consumption and sustenance such edible wheat, grain and coals and that such grain and flour be obtained at the market price of the district. And that if any be stored at the manors beyond the needs of the manors it shall be supplied to the household by the aforesaid writ of the steward and at a price fixed as before. Further when we are staying at any of our manors there should be no charge above the fixed price.

In addition we wish that our marshal is helpful and courteous and well-informed and knows each night how many meals are dispensed in hall and set liveries [board] and that no liveries are given without evidence and that every man of position is seated by right at table. Minstrels and messengers are below them and served according to their estate as well as the master of the household's servants. The waiters are ordered to come at once to serve in hall when we ourselves are seated and that they come all together so service proceeds in proper sequence. And foreign youths are seated together and served honourably according to their estate. And after eating when they rise they do not linger in the hall until the officers come, but go straight to their horses without creating a nuisance.

Further the marshal will rise each morning to return to duty and see if the pages or other strangers who often [?tear in MS] rise early are up to mischief before the main party are up. Then the marshal will go and see that the palfreys and other horses are free of litter or other filth that clings to animals. He does not deal just with the [?tear in MS] . . . palfreys but with all the horses of the household. He sees also that the mangers and troughs are supplied with provender and hay, not meanly nor wastefully by carelessness. And he decides when the farrier will shoe the horses and sees that the servants do not waste shoes other than what the farrier may order, and clerks' and squires' horses are done in proper order and not just at will. And we order that he shall be the first to rise and while the rest sleep he must be like the keeper (*hosebond*) of the household and in the evening see to the comfort of the horses as in the morning, and he will oversee the delivery of hay and grain and that all this is recorded on the account.

We will and command that he be not lax and does not overlook dogs and birds (*oysels*) which must be seized everyday and there can be no exceptions. He must not go out of earshot of the hostel without special authority of the steward and if summoned return in haste. Further we wish and command that separate suppers and dinners are not allowed to officers but that those who want dinner or supper will go to table in hall and have them in comfort. And after we leave hall having eaten and supped and after the grand officers (*granz mestres*) with their clerks and stewards have left it is ordered that the hall be closed for the use of officers assuming all have had enough without being extravagant.

And he should make enquiry in the neighbourhood of where we are staying that there is no nuisance to be had from single women or pages, and others who cannot be trusted or whom no one else can vouch for be speedily removed from within the privacy of the household. They can sow discord and make mischief. Further we order that between All Saints' eve and Easter eve there shall be a fire lit in hall. The dispensing of candles is at the discretion of the steward and marshal. At any time we come in summer or winter we stay up by candle light nor can officers be without candles, nor shall others that stay up with us be without a candle. In addition he must see that the hall is neatly furnished, benches well kept, as well as laver [jug] and basin and things pertaining to the hall.

And we wish that our butler of squire status shall be master of both pantry and buttery and that he see that the flour of which our bread is made is good, clean and pure, and that at each baking he makes two bushels of whiter and lighter bread than the common kind. And he shall see that the beer that he gives to us or to any of our clerks and reeves is good and in no way mixed. He also shall know how to be responsible to the steward for linen, towels, napkins and other minor things of the pantry, and hooped barrels, small casks or mugs when he has to sort them. Also he will have to account to the steward in writing as explained above and he will account at audit each night for the flour baked and how good it is in relation to the price of that used in the household. And he shall watch often over the mill and the baking. We wish further that he keep an eye on the brewing when necessary. And when beer has to be bought he shall do it himself and charge to account. In addition we wish that the key of the pantry and buttery shall never be far from their doors, but they are ready to honour the needs of the *Seygnor*. There shall be no issue by the pantryman nor those serving under him except by order and in the presence of the steward or marshal, and he shall in no way go any distance from the household without the special authority of the steward, and the keys of the two offices are in his charge every night and by day except when it is necessary for his assistants to carry out their duties under him.

And further we order that our master cook is chief keeper of our larder and he so organises it that there is no waste of anything in regard to the larder or kitchen. He will be clean and no one else shall approach our meat and it is our particular rule that no one be allowed into the kitchen who has not been assigned to the kitchen. He is responsible for the container (*la vessele*), issues in writing being made by the steward of the household. But for purchases of all things related to his office he may in no way go beyond necessary acquisitions without prior permission.

Further we order that he who carves before us be sober and clean in all ways, and that he pays special attention to our requirements and that he requests and knows which part we prefer if there be no special authority from ourselves. This man and our chamberlain we allow and no others into our chamber and its chapel for instructions when only ourselves and our chaplains are together there.

In addition we order that our porter may be sober, modest and polite to all and he should never be so rash as to leave the courtyard (*curt*) of the house where we are staying. He should examine the liveries to the hall when they pass his office and if he sees anything suspicious then he has the livery made known to the steward or marshal and warns the other porters not to let it pass, and searches what is carried and holds it until he has spoken with the marshal. He should not allow any container to be taken out of the gate, and keeps the house free of bawdy youths or women so that no harm can be done that may be brought to our notice. And if a stranger comes to the gate who is not known or identified that he be held at the gate in a courteous manner until it is known who he is and a message has been sent to the steward or marshal. And the laundress should stop at the gate and there receive the linen that is to be washed and make the exchange with the officers and servants of the clerks and others of the body (*meisnee*) of the household.

Further at bedtime the porter will visit the whole courtyard and see that no one remains within against our rules. And we will and command that neither for us nor for any other should he leave charge of the gate. And the porter knows about farriery and the craft of blacksmith which he will use in the morning or after eating when the hall will be empty so that one officer does not clash with another.

In addition we wish that our larderer can dress a larder as well with game as with normal meat and that for advice and guidance the master cook controls this post. And he knows how to respond to requests and outgoings and that in the absence of the master cook will be the principal in the kitchen. He should be modest and good-natured and be responsible to the master cook in whatever relates to his duties.

Then we wish that no one of our household should have a dog or bird and if anyone does bring in a dog or bird and keeps it for three days it is our ruling that he gives it to whomever we please. Further we rule that none of master's servants may have a manor horse, nor goes riding with one unless we give permission personally, and if any page has a horse the marshal banishes the page from our house and checks the origin of the horse after reproving the remover.

We wish that our marshal dresses up our squires in the morning and that he employs finer costume than normally used when we have to come before Parliament or assemblies where other *grans seignors* are present.

These are the people (*meisnez*) that we wish to have in the household: first our two chaplains whom we wish should be principally honoured after ourselves.

Now to gowns:

Our mother, a gown with appropriate fur

Our sister, a gown with fur

A master of the house (*logistr'*), two full gowns with fur, two horses, two servants, with straw for the two horses and each night of his stay half a bushel of grain and each working day a full bushel

Master Renald of St Albans, a full gown

A master of physic, the same conditions as the master of the house if he is stopping and not having full board on his rounds

A steward of our household, clerk with the same conditions as the master of the house and forty sous a year

The Steward of West Parts, two coloured gowns with lamb's wool and two horses

Jake de Senescahl, two coloured gowns

Thomas Romein, two coloured gowns

Master Adam de Carewell, one coloured gown

Two scholar nephews, two gowns

William Son of Hugh two gowns

Clerk of the manors one gown

Clerk of the Steward, one gown

Bailiff of Islip, two gowns with fur trimming

Clerk of the Chamber, one coloured gown

Due to the squires:

Steward of lands, two striped gowns (*de Raye*) with suitable fur and at Christmas four lambskins dyed and at Pentecost four lambskins dyed, and he can have three horses at his stops

Richard Vaus, two gowns, two horses

William de Wenloc, two gowns

William de Ewe, two gowns and a horse

A valet for our use, two gowns, one horse

A chief butler, two gowns, one horse

A master cook, two gowns, one horse

A marshal, two gowns, one horse, one fur, one gown

Bailiff of Pershore, two gowns

Bailiff of Staines, two gowns

Bailiff of Westminster, two gowns, one horse

Masters' servants (*Vadlez de mesters*):

A chamberlain, one gown and 4s

A larderer, one gown and half a mark

An under-butler, one gown, 4s

An under-pantryman, a robe, 4s

A porter, a gown and 4s

A baker and brewer, one gown and half mark

The carter one gown, 4s

The park-keeper of Pershore, one gown

The woodward of Islip, one gown

The warrener of Wick?, one gown

John Churchwine, one gown

Thomas le Jeofne, one gown
The barber, one apron? (*warnement*)
The servants:
A palfreyman one robe, 2s
A servant for the chaplain, one gown, 2s
A servant for the panniers, one gown, 3s
Two servants for the wagon, one gown each and 2s

Appendix IV
Abbots' and Priors' houses in London

Compiled from Stow's *Survey of London* and Dr Schofield's *Medieval London Houses* with further additions by Dr Schofield, who has pointed out that there were nine priories in London with resident heads. Donkin (1978) has found references to over a score of properties owned by Cistercian houses in London before 1300. They may have been rented out or used as offices, not as accommodation for heads of houses. It is probably wisest to regard the following list as a sample although certainly fuller than that in Appendix II.

Heads of houses with Parliamentary Duties:
Battle, Sussex. Tooley St; Southwark. Schofield No. 97
Bury St Edmunds, Suffolk. Aldgate. Large house according to Stow (1/186)
Canterbury, St Augustine's. Southwark. Acquired by 1215. Scho. 232
Cirencester Abbey (Augustinian). Fleet Street site acquired between 1133 and 1216. Schofield's letter 15 Dec 1999
Colchester, St John's Essex, Mincing Lane, about 1230. Letter from Schofield 15 Dec. 1999
Evesham, Worcs. Leadenhall St; Scho 117
Glastonbury, Som. West Southfield. Sch 187
Hyde, Winchester, Southwark Stow 2/53
Malmesbury, Wilts; Holborn. Purchased 1364. Schofield's letter 15 Dec. 1999
Ramsey, Hunts. Beech Lane. 'Great house' after Stow 1/302
Reading, Berks; purchased by 1212, parish of St Benet Sherehog moved to St Andrew by the Wardrobe *c*.1327. Schofield's letter 15 Dec. 1999
St Albans, Herts. Broad St. Purchased 1214. Sch 39
Tewkesbury, Glos. Bride Lane. From 1220. Scho 135
Waltham, Bishop's, Essex (Augustinian). St Mary Hill. Scho. 135
Winchcombe, Glos. Fleet St. Tenant from 1426. Schofield's letter 15/12/99
York, St Mary's. By 1421 in parish of St Dunstan in the East. After 1448 moved to site in Peter Lane. Schofield's letter 15 Dec. 1999

Houses of Heads of other Houses:
Canterbury, Christchurch, Prior of, Tooley St; Southwark. Scho 200
Chertsey, Thames St. Tenant from 1296-7. Scho. 163
Fécamp (*Fircamp*), Seine Inférieure (Norman coast). Large riverside messuage Stow 2/13
Lewes, Sussex (Cluniac). Tooley St; Southwark Scho. 199

Merton Priory, Oxon. (Augustinian), Tooley St; Southwark. Scho. 197
Nocton Priory, Lincs. (Augustinian), Chancery Lane Stow 2/43
Ogbourne St. George Priory. Wilts. Stow 2/13
Tortington Priory, Sussex (Augustinian). Walbrook. Stow 2/223
Walden, Saffron, Essex. Aldergate St Scho. 4
Waverley, Surrey (Cistercian). Southwark Stow 2/56

Appendix V
Monastic licences to crenellate

A: Augustinian; B: Benedictine; C: Cistercian; P: Premonstratensian
An asterisk (★) indicates a large gatehouse, of the relevant date, surviving wholly or partly.

Year	Site	Grantee	Enrolment	Work
1293 (Dec)	Halesowen Abbey, Worcs	Abbot and Convent, P	CPR, p.55	New chambers
1296 (Sep)	Tynemouth Priory, Northumberland	Prior and Convent, B (the great gate is from the next century)	CPR, 135	Crenellate
★1308 (Jul)	Peterborough Abbey	Abbot and Convent, B	CPR, 135	W. Gate and houses behind
★1308 (Oct)	Canterbury, St Augustines	A and C; B	CPR, 144	Chamber before gate
1318 (Jul)	York, St Marys	A and C; B	CPR, 190	Wall not over 16ft high
★1327 (Oct)	St Benet of Holme, Norfolk	A and C; B	CPR, 183	Wall abbey
1330 (Jul)	Abingdon Abbey, Oxon	A and C; B (the gate is of the next century)	CPR, 547	Wall abbey
★1332 (May)	Evesham Abbey, Worcs	A and C; B	CPR 283	House in front of gate
★1336 (Mar)	Evesham Abbey, Worcs	Abbot	CPR, 230	Extension of area
1337 (Oct)	Buckland Abbey, Devon	A and C; B	CPR, 529	Church and dwelling
★1338 (Jun)	Battle Abbey, Sussex	A and C; B	CPR, 92	Whole site
1344 (Jul)	Guisborough Priory, Yorks	P and C; A	CPR, 316	Dwelling
1345 (Aug)	Rochester Priory, Kent	P and C; A	CPR, 539	Wall site
★1346 (Sep)	Langley Abbey, Norfolk	A and C; P	CPR, 164	Belfry and crenellate

1348 (Mar)	Langdon Abbey, Kent,	A and C; P	CPR, 38	Gatehouse (*domum porte*)
★1348 (Jul)	Whalley Abbey, Lancs	A and C	CPR, 124	Church and close
1348 (Oct)	Wolsty (Wolmsty), Cumb S. of Silloth	Abbot of Holmcultram A (Abbeytown), C	CPR, 194	'Castle' ruin
★1357 (Jun)	St Albans Abbey	A and C; B	CPR, 574	Crenellate dwelling place
1360 (Jul)	Lewes Priory, Sussex	P and C, Cluniac	CPR, 444	Crenellate
1362 (Jul)	Drax Priory, Yorks	P and C, A	CPR, 237	Church and belfry
1365 (Oct)	Quarr Abbey, IOW	A and C, C	CPR, 168	Own premises and fish-house
★1366 (Apr)	Waltham Abbey, Essex	A and C, A	CPR, 309	Crenellate partly ruinous belfry
1367 (Oct)	Shaftesbury Abbey (Nunnery), Dorset	Abbess and C, B	CPR, 10	Church and belfry
★1369 (Feb)	Worcester Priory	P and C; B	CPR, 216	Priory buildings
★1369 (Apr)	Waltham Abbey, Essex	A and C; A	CPR, 245	Abbey
1373 (Mar)	Winchcombe Abbey,. Glos	A and C; B	CPR, 260	Abbey, houses
1375 (Nov)	Selby Abbey, Yorks (Great gate taken down in 1806)	A and C; B	CPR, 192	Church cloister, house
★1377 (Mar)	Chester St Werburghs Abbey	A and C, B	CPR, 442	Abbey
★1377 (Nov)	Chester St Werburghs Abbey	A and C, B	CPR, 56	Repeat
★1382 (Aug)	Thornton Abbey, Lincs	A and C, A	CPR, 166	New houses over and beside gate
★1388 (May)	Bridlington Priory, Yorks	P and C, A	CPR, 439	Priory
★1389 (May)	Thornton Abbey, Linc	A and C, A	CPR, 28	Crenellate abbey
1399 (Mar)	Manor houses at Ince, Little Sutton, and ★Saighton Grange, Ches.	St Werburgh's Chester A & C, B	CPR, 552	Crenellate
1410 (Feb)	As above	As above	CPR, 160	As above

Bibliography

The works listed are those referred to in the text but should provide a useful launch pad for those who wish to pursue the subject further.

Contemporary sources

Arnold, T. (ed.) 1892, *Annals of St Edmunds Abbey*, 3 cols, Rolls Series

Brewer, J.E. (ed.) 1846, *Chronicon monasterii de Bello*, London

Butler, H.E. (ed.) 1949, *The Chronicle of Jocelin of Brakelond*, London

Dugdale, W. 1817-30, *Monasticon Anglicanum*, ed. by T. Caley, H. Ellis, B. Bandinel, 9 vols, London

Dymond, D. (ed.) 1995-6, *Register of Thetford Priory*, 2 vols, British Academy

Fegan, E.S. (ed.) 1914, *The Journal of Prior William More*, Worcestershire Historical Society

Fowler, J.T. (ed.) 1903, *Rites of Durham*, Sturtees Society 107

Giles, T.A. (ed.) 1952-3, *Matthew Paris's English History from the Year 1235-1273*, 3 vols, Bohn's Library

Harvey, B. (ed.), 1965, *Documents illustrating the rule of Walter De Wenlock, Abbot of Westminster, 1283-1307*, London

Hockey, S.P. (ed.), 1975, *The account book of Beaulieu Abbey*, Camden Society 4th Ser; 10.

Knowles, D. (ed.), 1951, *Decreta Lanfranci*, London

Macray, W.D. (ed.), 1863, *Chronicon Abbatiae de Evesham*, Rolls Series

McCann, J.M. (ed.) 1952, *The Rule of St Benedict*, London

Mellows, W.T. 1947, *The last days of Peterborough monastery*, Northamptonshire Record Society 12

Powicke, F.M. (ed.), 1950, *Walter Daniel's Life of Ailred of Rievaulx*, London

Riley, H.T. (ed.), 1963-65, *Chronica monasterii, S. Albani Thomae, Walsingham, Historia Anglicana*, 2 vols, Rolls Series (ed.) 1965-69, *Gesta abbatum S Albani . . . A Thome Walsingham*, 3 vols, Rolls Series

Thompson, A.H. (ed), 1919, 1927, *Visitations of religious houses in the diocese of Lincoln*, 2 vols,. Canterbury and York Society

Stevenson, J. (ed.), 1957m *Chronicon Monasterii de Abingon*, Rolls Series

Veilleux, A. 1984, *La vie de Saint Pachome selon la tradition Copte,* Bagrelles-en-Mauges

Walcott, M.E.C. 1871, 'Inventories and valuations of religious houses at the time of the Dissolution from the Public Record Office', *Archaeologia* 43, 201-49

Modern works

Adeney, W.F. 1908, *The Greek and Eastern Churches*, Edinburgh

Atkinson, T.D. 1933, *An architectual history of the Benedictine monastery of St Ethelreda at Ely*, Cambridge

Aubert, M. 1947, *L'architecture cistercienne en France*, 2nd ed. 2 vols, Paris

Beckford, W. 1972, *Recollections of an excursion to the monasteries of Alcobaça and Batalha*. Ed. by B. Alexander. London

Biddle, M., Lambrick, H.T. & Mayers, J.N.L., 'The early history of Abbingdon, Berkshire and its abbey', *Medieval Archaeology* 12, 26-69

Brakspear, H., 'The abbot's house at Battle'. *Archaeologia,* 83, 137-166

Brayley, E.W. 1818, *The history and antiquities of the abbey church of St Peter*, *Westminster*. 2 vols, London

Capuani, M. 1988, *Monte Athos:baluardo monastico del Christinanesimo orientale,* Novara

Chew, H.M. 1932, *The English ecclesiastical tenants-in-chief and Knight Service*. Oxford

The Cloister Symposium. 1972, *Gesta, 12*

Colvin, H.M. 1951, *The White canons in England*. Oxford

Conant, K.J. 1968, *Cluny: les eglises st la maison du chef d'ordre*. Cambridge, Mass.

Coppack, G. 1986, 'Some descriptions of Rievaulx abbey in 1538-9 :the disposition of a major Cistercian precinct in the early sixteenth century' *Journal of the British Archaeological Association*, 139, 100-133

Cramp, R. 1969, 'Excavations at the Saxon monastic sites of Wearmouth and Jarrow, an interim report', *Medieval Archaeology* 13, 22-66

Cranage, D.S. 1922, 'The monastery of St Milburga at Much Wenlock', *Archaeologia* 72, 105-32

Crossley, F.H. 1949, *The English abbey*. 3rd ed. London

Donkin, R.K. 1978, *The Cistercians*: *Studies in the geography of medieval England and Wales*. Toronto

Elderern, B. van & Robinson, J.M. 1977, in Newsletter 99/100 of *American Research center in Egypt*

Emery, A. 1996, 2000, *Great medieval houses of England and Wales*. 2/3 vols published, Cambridge

Enlart, A. 1894, *Origines francaises de l'architecture en Italie*. Paris

Gilchrist, R. and Mytum H. (ed.) 1989, *The archaeology of rural monasteries*. British Archaeological Report 203

Gilyard-Beer, R. 1958, *Abbeys: an introduction to the religious houses of England and Wales*. HMSO

Gilyard-Beer, R. & Coppack, G. 1986, 'Excavations at Fountains Abbey, North Yorkshire 1979-80: The early development of the monastery' *Archaeologia*, 108, 147-87

Godfrey, W. 1930, 'The abbot's parlour, Thame Park', *Arch. Journ*. 59-68

Greene, J.P. 1989, *Norton Priory*. Cambridge

Grossman, P. 1979, 'The basilica of St Pachomius', *Biblical Archaeologist* 42, 232-36

Holton-Krayenbuhl, A. 1999, 'The prior's lodgings at Ely', *Arch. Journ*. 56, 294-342

Hope, W.H. St. J. 1900, 'Fountains Abbey, Yorks.', *Arch. Journ.* 15, 269-403

Hope, W.H. St. J. 1907, *Kirkstead Abbey*, Pub. Thoresby Soc. 16

Horn, W. 1973, 'On the origins of medieval cloister', *Gesta* 12, 13-52

Horn, W. and Born, E. 1979, *The plan of St Gall.* University of California Press, Berkeley, 3 vols

Jacobsen, W. 1992, *Der Klosterplan von St Gallen und die Karolingische Architektur.* Berlin

Keller, F. 1844, *Bauriss des Kloster St Gallen vom Jahre 820.* Zurich

Knowles, D. 1966, *The monastic order in England and the religious orders in England, vols. 1-4*, 2nd ed. Cambridge

Knowles 1965, *From Pachomius to Ignatius.* Oxford

Knowles & Hadcock, R.N. 1971, *Medieval Religious Houses in England.* London

Leclercq, J. 1974, *The love of learning and the desire for God.* 2nd ed. New York

Lefort, L.T. 1939, 'Les premiers monasteres pachomiens', *Museon* 52, 379-407

Luchaire, A. 1892, *Manuel des institutions francaises; periode des Capetiens directs.* Paris

Meer, F. van der & Mohrmann, C. 1958, *Atlas of the early Christian world.* Nelson, London

Morant, R.W. 1995, *The monastic gatehouse.* Lewes

Myers, J.N.L., 'Butley Priory, Suffolk', *Arch. J.* 90, 177-281

Pearce, E.H. 1920, *Walter de Wenlok, abbot of Westminster.* London

Peers, C. & Radford, C.A. 1943, 'The Saxon monastery of Whitby', *Archaeologia* 89, 27-88

Peigne-Delacourt, M. (ed.) 1882, *Dom Michel Germain (1645-94). Le Monasticon Gallicanum.* 2 vols, Paris

Platt, C. 1969, *The monastic grange.* London

Platt, C. 1984, *The abbeys and priories of medieval England.* London

Powell, E. 1896, *The rising in East Anglia in 1381.* Cambridge

Powell, J.E. & Wallis, K. 1968, *The House of Lords in the middle ages: a history of the English House of Lords.* London

Robinson, J.A. 1911, *The abbot's house at Westminster.* London

Robinson, J.A. 1911, *Gilbert Crispin, abbot of Westminster: a study of the abbey under Norman rule.* London

Rousseau, J.A. 1985, *Pachomius: the making of a community in the fourth century.* Egypt, University of California, Berkeley

Rutton, L. 1910, 'The manor of Eia or Eye next Westminister', *Archaeologia* 62, Pt 1, 31-50

Schofield, J. 1995, *Medieval London Houses.* Yale University Press

Sloane, B. 1999, 'Reversing the Dissolution: reconstructing London's medieval monasteries', *Trans. London & Middx. Arch. Soc.* 50, 67-77

Southern, R.W. 1970, *Western Society and the Church in the middle ages.* London

Stow, J. 1908, *Survey of London.* ed. by C.L. Kingsford, 2 vols. London

Thompson, A.H., 1930, *Bolton Priory*, Pub. Thoresby Soc. 30

Thompson, M.W. 1981, *Ruins: their preservation and display.* British Museum Publications

Thompson, M.W. 1992, 'Keep or country house: thin walled Norman proto-keeps', *Fortress*, 13-22

Thompson, M.W. 1995, *The medieval hall.* Aldershot

Thompson, M.W. 1998, *Medieval bishops' houses in England and Wales.* Aldershot

Veilleux, A. 1968, *La liturgie dans le cenobetisme pachomien.* Studiensa Anselmiensa 57

Viollet-le-Duc, E. 1875, *Dictionnaire raisonné de l'architecture francaise du xie au xvie siècle.* 10 vols. Paris

Westflake, H.F. 1921, *Westminster Abbey: the last days of the monastery as shown by the life and times of Abbot John Islip.* London

Westflake, H.F. 1923, *Westminster Abbey.* 2 vols. London

Widmore, R. 1751, *An history of the church of St Peter, Westminster, commonly called Westminster Abbey chiefly from manuscript sources.* London

Wilcox, R. 1982, 'Thetford Cluniac Priory: excavations 1971-77', *Norfolk Archaeology* 40, 1-18

Willis, B. 1718, *An history of the mitred Parliamentary abbies and conventual cathedral churches.* 2 vols. London

Willis, R. 1848, 'Description of the ancient plan of the monastery of St Gall', *Arch. Journ.* 5, 85-117

Workman, H.B. 1913, *The evolution of the monastic ideal from the earliest times to the coming of the friars.* London

Yates, K. 1843, *History and antiquities of the abbey of St Edmundsbury.* 2nd ed. London

Glossary

Most of the terms used are explained in the text, particularly the monastic orders, but it may be useful to the reader to redefine some of them, particularly architectural terms, some of the more obscure having been deliberately avoided.

Abbey	The higher of the two grades of monastery ruled by an abbot as opposed to the lower grade of priory ruled by a prior.
Aisle	The longitudinal divisions of a building created by arcades along its length, particularly the side divisions, the central wider division being often called the nave or vessel.
Almonry	A building near the entry from which alms were distributed.
Apse	A curved projection from a church enclosing an altar or chapel.
Asperge	The sprinkling of the rooms around the cloister with holy water during the Sunday procession.
Barbican	Flanking walls in front of a gateway to constrict the entry against an approaching hostile body, only occurring at Thornton gatehouse.
Basilica	The great aisled building of Roman times from which the plan of greater western churches was derived and so called by this name.
Black friars	Dominican friars so nicknamed by the colour of their habit.
Canons regular	Living more or less as monks but by the Augustinian, not the Benedictine rule.
Cellarer	The monastic officer responsible for stores and much else who gave his name to the west range although he did not control it.
Censer	The incensing of parts of the cloister in the Sunday procession.
Chapter house	The very important building in the east range where the whole body of religious met daily to conduct business and administer punishment.
Day stairs	The stairs leading from the east alley to the dormitory for daytime access.
Frater	See refectory.
Garth	The area enclosed within the cloister usually a lawn or garden and sometimes containing a fountain or lavabo.
Grange	A farm run by monks, usually Cistercian, not by tenants.
Grey friars	Franciscan friars so nicknamed because of the colour of their habit.

Hall	A large hall used principally for eating at the centre of a lay household.
Infirmary	A large, often aisled, building outside the cloister on the east side used as a hospital for sick and elderly monks.
Laura	The building with cells for sleeping used in early and Greek monasteries in no definite relationship to the church.
Lavabo	The wash place near the frater either formed by a trough in the wall or a free-standing basin in the garth.
Lay Brother	He had taken the monastic vows but was not a quire monk but employed in their service, being extensively used by the Cistercians.
Licence to crenellate	The issue of such a licence to fortify a building is recorded on the back of the Patent Rolls.
Mansio	The abbot's hostel presumably for guest monks shown on the St Gall plan as a two-storeyed building with its own services.
Misericord	The building designed for blood-letting by the monks.
Nave	The main body of the church west of the transept crossing to which the cloister was attached on the south or north side.
Night stairs	The stairs descending at the end of the dormitory into the church transept giving ready access to the quire and used for early morning offices without entering the cloister.
Obedientary	Monastic officer.
Oratory	A place for private prayer.
Offices	The eight periods of sung prayer in quire.
Order of monks	Originally monasteries were independent of each other but with reform movements there developed control from the place of reform the monks of the new monasteries wearing the same habit and following the same way of life throughout houses of the new Order. So the Cistercian monks owed allegiance to Citeaux, the Carthusians to Chartreuse and so on.
Paradise	The lunate enclosures around the apses on the St Gall plan.
Parlours	The rooms where talking was allowed, either at the entry at the end of the west range adjoining the church (outer parlour) or adjoining the chapter house in the east range (inner parlour).
Portcullis	Spiked grill moving vertically in grooves to close an entry, found in some monastic gatehouses.
Prior	The second in command in an abbey or head of a priory or of the convent in a monastic cathedral.
Priory	A lower grade of monastery than an abbey and ruled by a prior.
Quire or choir	The arrangements of stalls (seats) at or near the crossing in the church where the monks chanted the daily offices.
Refectory	Often called the frater in contemporary sources, the dining hall with its pulpitum or raised reading desk from which sacred texts were read aloud during meals.

Rule From the time of Pachomius regular clergy, monks, lived by a Rule. There were many but the Rule of St Benedict was normal in the west or of St Basil in the east.

Solarium A private room shown on the first floor in the abbot's house in the St Gall plan.

Transepts The lateral arms of a cruciform church to one of which the east range of the cloister was attached, the point of their intersection with the church being called the crossing.

Vault Arched stone cover beneath wooden roof, or floor of upper chamber, of varying forms at different periods.

Warming room The only heated part of the cloister, under the dormitory in Benedictine cloisters, between the refectory and the east range in Cistercian cloisters.

Wicket A pedestrian doorway either inserted in the main gates or in monastic gatehouses constructed separately adjoining them.

Index

Page numbers in **bold** denote illustrations. Place names are usually those of a monastery or monastic manor.